T0107114

The Man-Made World

The Man-Made World

Charlotte Perkins Gilman

MINT EDITIONS

The Man-Made World was first published in 1911.

This edition published by Mint Editions 2020.

ISBN 9781513220451 | E-ISBN 9781513274829

Published by Mint Editions®

 MINT
EDITIONS
minteditionbooks.com

Publishing Director: Jennifer Newens
Design & Production: Rachel Lopez Metzger
Typesetting: Westchester Publishing Services

Contents

I

As to Humanness

Let us begin, inoffensively, with sheep. The sheep is a beast with which we are all familiar, being much used in religious imagery; the common stock of painters; a staple article of diet; one of our main sources of clothing; and an everyday symbol of bashfulness and stupidity.

In some grazing regions the sheep is an object of terror, destroying grass, bush and forest by omnipresent nibbling; on the great plains, sheep-keeping frequently results in insanity, owing to the loneliness of the shepherd, and the monotonous appearance and behavior of the sheep.

By the poet, young sheep are preferred, the lamb gambolling gaily; unless it be in hymns, where "all we like sheep" are repeatedly described, and much stress is laid upon the straying propensities of the animal.

To the scientific mind there is special interest in the sequacity of sheep, their habit of following one another with automatic imitation. This instinct, we are told, has been developed by ages of wild crowded racing on narrow ledges, along precipices, chasms, around sudden spurs and corners, only the leader seeing when, where and how to jump. If those behind jumped exactly as he did, they lived. If they stopped to exercise independent judgment, they were pushed off and perished; they and their judgment with them.

All these things, and many that are similar, occur to us when we think of sheep. They are also ewes and rams. Yes, truly; but what of it? All that has been said was said of sheep, *genus ovis*, that bland beast, compound of mutton, wool, and foolishness so widely known. If we think of the sheep-dog (and dog-ess), the shepherd (and shepherd-ess), of the ferocious sheep-eating bird of New Zealand, the Kea (and Kea-ess), all these herd, guard, or kill the sheep, both rams and ewes alike. In regard to mutton, to wool, to general character, we think only of their sheepishness, not at all of their ramishness or eweishness. That which is ovine or bovine, canine, feline or equine, is easily recognized as distinguishing that particular species of animal, and has no relation whatever to the sex thereof.

Returning to our muttons, let us consider the ram, and wherein his character differs from the sheep. We find he has a more quarrelsome disposition. He paws the earth and makes a noise. He has a tendency to butt. So has a goat—Mr. Goat. So has Mr. Buffalo, and Mr. Moose, and Mr. Antelope. This tendency to plunge head foremost at an adversary—and to find any other gentleman an adversary on sight—evidently does not pertain to sheep, to *genus ovis;* but to any male creature with horns.

As "function comes before organ," we may even give a reminiscent glance down the long path of evolution, and see how the mere act of butting—passionately and perpetually repeated—born of the belligerent spirit of the male—produced horns!

The ewe, on the other hand, exhibits love and care for her little ones, gives them milk and tries to guard them. But so does a goat—Mrs. Goat. So does Mrs. Buffalo and the rest. Evidently this mother instinct is no peculiarity of *genus ovis,* but of any female creature.

Even the bird, though not a mammal, shows the same mother-love and mother-care, while the father bird, though not a butter, fights with beak and wing and spur. His competition is more effective through display. The wish to please, the need to please, the overmastering necessity upon him that he secure the favor of the female, has made the male bird blossom like a butterfly. He blazes in gorgeous plumage, rears haughty crests and combs, shows drooping wattles and dangling blobs such as the turkey-cock affords; long splendid feathers for pure ornament appear upon him; what in her is a mere tail-effect becomes in him a mass of glittering drapery.

Partridge-cock, farmyard-cock, peacock, from sparrow to ostrich, observe his mien! To strut and languish; to exhibit every beauteous lure; to sacrifice ease, comfort, speed, everything—to beauty—for her sake—this is the nature of the he-bird of any species; the characteristic, not of the turkey, but of the cock! With drumming of loud wings, with crow and quack and bursts of glorious song, he woos his mate; displays his splendors before her; fights fiercely with his rivals. To butt—to strut—to make a noise—all for love's sake; these acts are common to the male.

We may now generalize and clearly state: That is masculine which belongs to the male—to any or all males, irrespective of species. That is feminine which belongs to the female, to any or all females, irrespective of species. That is ovine, bovine, feline, canine, equine or asinine which belongs to that species, irrespective of sex.

In our own species all this is changed. We have been so taken up with the phenomena of masculinity and femininity, that our common humanity has largely escaped notice. We know we are human, naturally, and are very proud of it; but we do not consider in what our humanness consists; nor how men and women may fall short of it, or overstep its bounds, in continual insistence upon their special differences. It is "manly" to do this; it is "womanly" to do that; but what a human being should do under the circumstances is not thought of.

The only time when we do recognize what we call "common humanity" is in extreme cases, matters of life and death; when either man or woman is expected to behave as if they were also human creatures. Since the range of feeling and action proper to humanity, as such, is far wider than that proper to either sex, it seems at first somewhat remarkable that we have given it so little recognition.

A little classification will help us here. We have certain qualities in common with inanimate matter, such as weight, opacity, resilience. It is clear that these are not human. We have other qualities in common with all forms of life; cellular construction, for instance, the reproduction of cells and the need of nutrition. These again are not human. We have others, many others, common to the higher mammals; which are not exclusively ours—are not distinctively "human." What then are true human characteristics? In what way is the human species distinguished from all other species?

Our human-ness is seen most clearly in three main lines: it is mechanical, psychical and social. Our power to make and use things is essentially human; we alone have extra-physical tools. We have added to our teeth the knife, sword, scissors, mowing machine; to our claws the spade, harrow, plough, drill, dredge. We are a protean creature, using the larger brain power through a wide variety of changing weapons. This is one of our main and vital distinctions. Ancient animal races are traced and known by mere bones and shells, ancient human races by their buildings, tools and utensils.

That degree of development which gives us the human mind is a clear distinction of race. The savage who can count a hundred is more human than the savage who can count ten.

More prominent than either of these is the social nature of humanity. We are by no means the only group-animal; that ancient type of industry the ant, and even the well-worn bee, are social creatures. But insects of their kind are found living alone. Human beings never. Our human-ness begins with some low form of social relation and increases as that relation develops.

Human life of any sort is dependent upon what Kropotkin calls "mutual aid," and human progress keeps step absolutely with that interchange of specialized services which makes society organic. The nomad, living on cattle as ants live on theirs, is less human than the farmer, raising food by intelligently applied labor; and the extension of trade and commerce, from mere village market-places to the world-exchanges of to-day, is extension of human-ness as well.

Humanity, thus considered, is not a thing made at once and unchangeable, but a stage of development; and is still, as Wells describes it, "in the making." Our human-ness is seen to lie not so much in what we are individually, as in our relations to one another; and even that individuality is but the result of our relations to one another. It is in what we do and how we do it, rather than in what we are. Some, philosophically inclined, exalt "being" over "doing." To them this question may be put: "Can you mention any form of life that merely 'is,' without doing anything?"

Taken separately and physically, we are animals, *genus homo*; taken socially and psychically, we are, in varying degree, human; and our real history lies in the development of this human-ness.

Our historic period is not very long. Real written history only goes back a few thousand years, beginning with the stone records of ancient Egypt. During this period we have had almost universally what is here called an Androcentric Culture. The history, such as it was, was made and written by men.

The mental, the mechanical, the social development, was almost wholly theirs. We have, so far, lived and suffered and died in a man-made world. So general, so unbroken, has been this condition, that to mention it arouses no more remark than the statement of a natural law. We have taken it for granted, since the dawn of civilization, that "mankind" meant men-kind, and the world was theirs.

Women we have sharply delimited. Women were a sex, "the sex," according to chivalrous toasts; they were set apart for special services peculiar to femininity. As one English scientist put it, in 1888, "Women are not only not the race—they are not even half the race, but a subspecies told off for reproduction only."

This mental attitude toward women is even more clearly expressed by Mr. H. B. Marriot-Watson in his article on "The American Woman" in the "Nineteenth Century" for June, 1904, where he says: "Her constitutional restlessness has caused her to abdicate those functions which alone excuse or explain her existence." This is a peculiarly happy and condensed expression of the relative position of women during our androcentric culture. The man was accepted as the race type without one dissentient voice; and the woman—a strange, diverse creature, quite disharmonious in the accepted scheme of things—was excused and explained only as a female.

She has needed volumes of such excuse and explanation; also, apparently, volumes of abuse and condemnation. In any library catalogue we may find books upon books about women: physiological, sentimental, didactic, religious—all manner of books about women, as such. Even to-day in the works of Marholm—poor young Weininger, Moebius, and others, we find the same perpetual discussion of women—as such.

This is a book about men—as such. It differentiates between the human nature and the sex nature. It will not go so far as to allege man's masculine traits to be all that excuse, or explain his existence: but it will point out what are masculine traits as distinct from human ones, and what has been the effect on our human life of the unbridled dominance of one sex.

We can see at once, glaringly, what would have been the result of giving all human affairs into female hands. Such an extraordinary and deplorable situation would have "feminized" the world. We should have all become "effeminate."

See how in our use of language the case is clearly shown. The adjectives and derivatives based on woman's distinctions are alien and derogatory when applied to human affairs; "effeminate"—too female, connotes contempt, but has no masculine analogue; whereas "emasculate"—not enough male, is a term of reproach, and has no feminine analogue. "Virile"—manly, we oppose to "puerile"—childish, and the very word "virtue" is derived from "vir"—a man.

Even in the naming of other animals we have taken the male as the race type, and put on a special termination to indicate "his female," as in lion, lioness; leopard, leopardess; while all our human scheme of things rests on the same tacit assumption; man being held the human type; woman a sort of accompaniment and subordinate assistant, merely essential to the making of people.

She has held always the place of a preposition in relation to man. She has been considered above him or below him, before him, behind him, beside him, a wholly relative existence—"Sydney's sister," "Pembroke's mother"—but never by any chance Sydney or Pembroke herself.

Acting on this assumption, all human standards have been based on male characteristics, and when we wish to praise the work of a woman, we say she has "a masculine mind."

It is no easy matter to deny or reverse a universal assumption. The human mind has had a good many jolts since it began to think, but after each upheaval it settles down as peacefully as the vine-growers on Vesuvius, accepting the last lava crust as permanent ground.

What we see immediately around us, what we are born into and grow up with, be it mental furniture or physical, we assume to be the order of nature.

If a given idea has been held in the human mind for many generations, as almost all our common ideas have, it takes sincere and continued effort to remove it; and if it is one of the oldest we have in stock, one of the big, common, unquestioned world ideas, vast is the labor of those who seek to change it.

Nevertheless, if the matter is one of importance, if the previous idea was a palpable error, of large and evil effect, and if the new one is true and widely important, the effort is worth making.

The task here undertaken is of this sort. It seeks to show that what we have all this time called "human nature" and deprecated, was in great part only male nature, and good enough in its place; that what we have called "masculine" and admired as such, was in large part human, and should be applied to both sexes: that what we have called "feminine" and condemned, was also largely human and applicable to both. Our androcentric culture is so shown to have been, and still to be, a masculine culture in excess, and therefore undesirable.

In the preliminary work of approaching these facts it will be well to explain how it can be that so wide and serious an error should have been made by practically all men. The reason is simply that they were men. They were males, avid saw women as females—and not otherwise.

So absolute is this conviction that the man who reads will say, "Of course! How else are we to look at women except as females? They are females, aren't they?" Yes, they are, as men are males unquestionably; but there is possible the frame of mind of the old marquise who was asked by an English friend how she could bear to have the footman serve her breakfast in bed—to have a man in her bed-chamber—and replied sincerely, "Call you that thing there a man?"

The world is full of men, but their principal occupation is human work of some sort; and women see in them the human distinction preponderantly. Occasionally some unhappy lady marries her coachman—long contemplation of broad shoulders having an effect, apparently; but in general women see the human creature most; the male creature only when they love.

To the man, the whole world was his world; his because he was male; and the whole world of woman was the home; because she was female. She had her prescribed sphere, strictly limited to her feminine occupations and interests; he had all the rest of life; and not only so, but, having it, insisted on calling it male.

This accounts for the general attitude of men toward the now rapid humanization of women. From her first faint struggles toward freedom and justice, to her present valiant efforts toward full economic and political equality, each step has been termed "unfeminine" and resented as an intrusion upon man's place and power. Here shows the need of our new classification, of the three distinct fields of life—masculine, feminine and human.

As a matter of fact, there is a "woman's sphere," sharply defined and quite different from his; there is also a "man's sphere," as sharply defined and even more limited; but there remains a common sphere—that of humanity, which belongs to both alike.

In the earlier part of what is known as "the woman's movement," it was sharply opposed on the ground that women would become "unsexed." Let us note in passing that they have become unsexed in one particular, most glaringly so, and that no one has noticed or objected to it.

As part of our androcentric culture we may point to the peculiar reversal of sex characteristics which make the human female carry the burden of ornament. She alone, of all human creatures, has adopted the essentially masculine attribute of special sex-decoration; she does not fight for her mate as yet, but she blooms forth as the peacock and bird of paradise, in poignant reversal of nature's laws, even wearing masculine feathers to further her feminine ends.

Woman's natural work as a female is that of the mother; man's natural work as a male is that of the father; their mutual relation to this end being a source of joy and well-being when rightly held: but human work covers all our life outside of these specialties. Every handicraft, every profession, every science, every art, all normal amusements and recreations, all government, education, religion; the whole living world of human achievement: all this is human.

That one sex should have monopolized all human activities, called them "man's work," and managed them as such, is what is meant by the phrase "Androcentric Culture."

II

The Man-Made Family

The family is older than humanity, and therefore cannot be called a human institution. A post office, now, is wholly human; no other creature has a post office, but there are families in plenty among birds and beasts; all kinds permanent and transient; monogamous, polygamous and polyandrous.

We are now to consider the growth of the family in humanity; what is its rational development in humanness; in mechanical, mental and social lines; in the extension of love and service; and the effect upon it of this strange new arrangement—a masculine proprietor.

Like all natural institutions the family has a purpose; and is to be measured primarily as it serves that purpose; which is, the care and nurture of the young. To protect the helpless little ones, to feed and shelter them, to ensure them the benefits of an ever longer period of immaturity, and so to improve the race—this is the original purpose of the family.

When a natural institution becomes human it enters the plane of consciousness. We think about it; and, in our strange new power of voluntary action do things to it. We have done strange things to the family; or, more specifically, men have.

Balsac, at his bitterest, observed, "Women's virtue is man's best invention." Balsac was wrong. Virtue—the unswerving devotion to one mate—is common among birds and some of the higher mammals. If Balsac meant celibacy when he said virtue, why that is one of man's inventions—though hardly his best.

What man has done to the family, speaking broadly, is to change it from an institution for the best service of the child to one modified to his own service, the vehicle of his comfort, power and pride.

Among the heavy millions of the stirred East, a child—necessarily a male child—is desired for the credit and glory of the father, and his fathers; in place of seeing that all a parent is for is the best service of the child. Ancestor worship, that gross reversal of all natural law, is of wholly androcentric origin. It is strongest among old patriarchal races; lingers on in feudal Europe; is to be traced even in America today in a few sporadic efforts to magnify the deeds of our ancestors.

The best thing any of us can do for our ancestors is to be better than they were; and we ought to give our minds to it. When we use our past merely as a guide-book, and concentrate our noble emotions on the present and future, we shall improve more rapidly.

The peculiar changes brought about in family life by the predominance of the male are easily traced. In these studies we must keep clearly in mind the basic masculine characteristics: desire, combat, self-expression—all legitimate and right in proper use; only mischievous when excessive or out of place. Through them the male is led to strenuous competition for the favor of the female; in the overflowing ardours of song, as in nightingale and tomcat; in wasteful splendor of personal decoration, from the pheasant's breast to an embroidered waistcoat; and in direct struggle for the prize, from the stag's locked horns to the clashing spears of the tournament.

It is earnestly hoped that no reader will take offence at the necessarily frequent, reference to these essential features of maleness. In the many books about women it is, naturally, their femaleness that has been studied and enlarged upon. And though women, after thousands of years of such discussion, have become a little restive under the constant use of the word female: men, as rational beings, should not object to an analogous study—at least not for some time—a few centuries or so.

How, then, do we find these masculine tendencies, desire, combat and self-expression, affect the home and family when given too much power?

First comes the effect in the preliminary work of selection. One of the most uplifting forces of nature is that of sex selection. The males, numerous, varied, pouring a flood of energy into wide modifications, compete for the female, and she selects the victor, this securing to the race the new improvements.

In forming the proprietary family there is no such competition, no such selection. The man, by violence or by purchase, does the choosing—he selects the kind of woman that pleases him. Nature did not intend him to select; he is not good at it. Neither was the female intended to compete—she is not good at it.

If there is a race between males for a mate—the swiftest gets her first; but if one male is chasing a number of females he gets the slowest first. The one method improves our speed: the other does not. If males struggle and fight with one another for a mate, the strongest secures

CHARLOTTE PERKINS GILMAN

her; if the male struggles and fights with the female—(a peculiar and unnatural horror, known only among human beings) he most readily secures the weakest. The one method improves our strength—the other does not.

When women became the property of men; sold and bartered; "given away" by their paternal owner to their marital owner; they lost this prerogative of the female, this primal duty of selection. The males were no longer improved by their natural competition for the female; and the females were not improved; because the male did not select for points of racial superiority, but for such qualities as pleased him.

There is a locality in northern Africa, where young girls are deliberately fed with a certain oily seed, to make them fat,—that they may be the more readily married,—as the men like fat wives. Among certain more savage African tribes the chief's wives are prepared for him by being kept in small dark huts and fed on "mealies" and molasses; precisely as a Strasbourg goose is fattened for the gourmand. Now fatness is not a desirable race characteristic; it does not add to the woman's happiness or efficiency; or to the child's; it is merely an accessory pleasant to the master; his attitude being much as the amorous monad ecstatically puts it, in Sill's quaint poem, "Five Lives,"

> *"O the little female monad's lips!*
> *O the little female monad's eyes!*
> *O the little, little, female, female monad!"*

This ultra littleness and ultra femaleness has been demanded and produced by our Androcentric Culture.

Following this, and part of it, comes the effect on motherhood. This function was the original and legitimate base of family life; and its ample sustaining power throughout the long early period of "the mother-right;" or as we call it, the matriarchate; the father being her assistant in the great work. The patriarchate, with its proprietary family, changed this altogether; the woman, as the property of the man was considered first and foremost as a means of pleasure to him; and while she was still valued as a mother, it was in a tributary capacity. Her children were now his; his property, as she was; the whole enginery of the family was turned from its true use to this new one, hitherto unknown, the service of the adult male.

To this day we are living under the influence of the proprietary family. The duty of the wife is held to involve man-service as well as child-service, and indeed far more; as the duty of the wife to the husband quite transcends the duty of the mother to the child.

See for instance the English wife staying with her husband in India and sending the children home to be brought up; because India is bad for children. See our common law that the man decides the place of residence; if the wife refuses to go with him to howsoever unfit a place for her and for the little ones, such refusal on her part constitutes "desertion" and is ground for divorce.

See again the idea that the wife must remain with the husband though a drunkard, or diseased; regardless of the sin against the child involved in such a relation. Public feeling on these matters is indeed changing; but as a whole the ideals of the man-made family still obtain.

The effect of this on the woman has been inevitably to weaken and overshadow her sense of the real purpose of the family; of the relentless responsibilities of her duty as a mother. She is first taught duty to her parents, with heavy religious sanction; and then duty to her husband, similarly buttressed; but her duty to her children has been left to instinct. She is not taught in girlhood as to her preeminent power and duty as a mother; her young ideals are all of devotion to the lover and husband: with only the vaguest sense of results.

The young girl is reared in what we call "innocence;" poetically described as "bloom;" and this condition is held one of her chief "charms." The requisite is wholly androcentric. This "innocence" does not enable her to choose a husband wisely; she does not even know the dangers that possibly confront her. We vaguely imagine that her father or brother, who do know, will protect her. Unfortunately the father and brother, under our current "double standard" of morality do not judge the applicants as she would if she knew the nature of their offenses.

Furthermore, if her heart is set on one of them, no amount of general advice and opposition serves to prevent her marrying him. "I love him!" she says, sublimely. "I do not care what he has done. I will forgive him. I will save him!"

This state of mind serves to forward the interests of the lover, but is of no advantage to the children. We have magnified the duties of the wife, and minified the duties of the mother; and this is inevitable in a family relation every law and custom of which is arranged from the masculine viewpoint.

From this same viewpoint, equally essential to the proprietary family, comes the requirement that the woman shall serve the man. Her service is not that of the associate and equal, as when she joins him in his business. It is not that of a beneficial combination, as when she practices another business and they share the profits; it is not even that of the specialist, as the service of a tailor or barber; it is personal service—the work of a servant.

In large generalization, the women of the world cook and wash, sweep and dust, sew and mend, for the men.

We are so accustomed to this relation; have held it for so long to be the "natural" relation, that it is difficult indeed to show that it is distinctly unnatural and injurious. The father expects to be served by the daughter, a service quite different from what he expects of the son. This shows at once that such service is no integral part of motherhood, or even of marriage; but is supposed to be the proper industrial position of women, as such.

Why is this so? Why, on the face of it, given a daughter and a son, should a form of service be expected of the one, which would be considered ignominious by the other?

The underlying reason is this. Industry, at its base, is a feminine function. The surplus energy of the mother does not manifest itself in noise, or combat, or display, but in productive industry. Because of her mother-power she became the first inventor and laborer; being in truth the mother of all industry as well as all people.

Man's entrance upon industry is late and reluctant; as will be shown later in treating his effect on economics. In this field of family life, his effect was as follows:

Establishing the proprietary family at an age when the industry was primitive and domestic; and thereafter confining the woman solely to the domestic area, he thereby confined her to primitive industry. The domestic industries, in the hands of women, constitute a survival of our remotest past. Such work was "woman's work" as was all the work then known; such work is still considered woman's work because they have been prevented from doing any other.

The term "domestic industry" does not define a certain kind of labor, but a certain grade of labor. Architecture was a domestic industry once—when every savage mother set up her own tepee. To be confined to domestic industry is no proper distinction of womanhood; it is an historic distinction, an economic distinction, it sets a date and limit to woman's industrial progress.

In this respect the man-made family has resulted in arresting the development of half the field. We have a world wherein men, industrially, live in the twentieth century; and women, industrially, live in the first—and back of it.

To the same source we trace the social and educational limitations set about women. The dominant male, holding his women as property, and fiercely jealous of them, considering them always as *his*, not belonging to themselves, their children, or the world; has hedged them in with restrictions of a thousand sorts; physical, as in the crippled Chinese lady or the imprisoned odalisque; moral, as in the oppressive doctrines of submission taught by all our androcentric religions; mental, as in the enforced ignorance from which women are now so swiftly emerging.

This abnormal restriction of women has necessarily injured motherhood. The man, free, growing in the world's growth, has mounted with the centuries, filling an ever wider range of world activities. The woman, bound, has not so grown; and the child is born to a progressive fatherhood and a stationary motherhood. Thus the man-made family reacts unfavorably upon the child. We rob our children of half their social heredity by keeping the mother in an inferior position; however legalized, hallowed, or ossified by time, the position of a domestic servant is inferior.

It is for this reason that child culture is at so low a level, and for the most part utterly unknown. Today, when the forces of education are steadily working nearer to the cradle, a new sense is wakening of the importance of the period of infancy, and its wiser treatment; yet those who know of such a movement are few, and of them some are content to earn easy praise—and pay—by belittling right progress to gratify the prejudices of the ignorant.

The whole position is simple and clear; and easily traceable to its root. Given a proprietary family, where the man holds the woman primarily for his satisfaction and service—then necessarily he shuts her up and keeps her for these purposes. Being so kept, she cannot develop humanly, as he has, through social contact, social service, true social life. (We may note in passing, her passionate fondness for the child-game called "society" she has been allowed to entertain herself withal; that poor simiacrum of real social life, in which people decorate themselves and madly crowd together, chattering, for what is called "entertainment.") Thus checked in social development, we have but a low grade motherhood to offer our children; and the children, reared in the primitive conditions thus artificially maintained, enter life with a false perspective, not only toward men and women, but toward life as a whole.

The child should receive in the family, full preparation for his relation to the world at large. His whole life must be spent in the world, serving it well or ill; and youth is the time to learn how. But the androcentric home cannot teach him. We live to-day in a democracy-the man-made family is a despotism. It may be a weak one; the despot may be dethroned and overmastered by his little harem of one; but in that case she becomes the despot—that is all. The male is esteemed "the head of the family;" it belongs to him; he maintains it; and the rest of the world is a wide hunting ground and battlefield wherein he competes with other males as of old.

The girl-child, peering out, sees this forbidden field as belonging wholly to men-kind; and her relation to it is to secure one for herself—not only that she may love, but that she may live. He will feed, clothe and adorn her—she will serve him; from the subjection of the daughter to that of the wife she steps; from one home to the other, and never enters the world at all—man's world.

The boy, on the other hand, considers the home as a place of women, an inferior place, and longs to grow up and leave it—for the real world. He is quite right. The error is that this great social instinct, calling for full social exercise, exchange, service, is considered masculine, whereas it is human, and belongs to boy and girl alike.

The child is affected first through the retarded development of his mother, then through the arrested condition of home industry; and further through the wrong ideals which have arisen from these conditions. A normal home, where there was human equality between mother and father, would have a better influence.

We must not overlook the effect of the proprietary family on the proprietor himself. He, too, has been held back somewhat by this reactionary force. In the process of becoming human we must learn to recognize justice, freedom, human rights; we must learn self-control and to think of others; have minds that grow and broaden rationally; we must learn the broad mutual interservice and unbounded joy of social intercourse and service. The petty despot of the man-made home is hindered in his humanness by too much manness.

For each man to have one whole woman to cook for and wait upon him is a poor education for democracy. The boy with a servile mother, the man with a servile wife, cannot reach the sense of equal rights we need to-day. Too constant consideration of the master's tastes makes the master selfish; and the assault upon his heart direct, or through that proverbial side-avenue, the stomach, which the dependent woman needs must make when she wants anything, is bad for the man, as well as for her.

We are slowly forming a nobler type of family; the union of two, based on love and recognized by law, maintained because of its happiness and use. We are even now approaching a tenderness and permanence of love, high pure enduring love; combined with the broad deep-rooted friendliness and comradeship of equals; which promises us more happiness in marriage than we have yet known. It will be good for all the parties concerned—man, woman and child: and promote our general social progress admirably.

If it needs "a head" it will elect a chairman pro tem. Friendship does not need "a head." Love does not need "a head." Why should a family?

III

Health and Beauty

Note—The word "Androcentric" we owe to Prof. Lester F. Ward. In his book, "Pure Sociology," Chap. 14, he describes the Androcentric Theory of life, hitherto universally accepted; and introduces his own "Gyneacocentric Theory." All who are interested in the deeper scientific aspects of this question are urged to read that chapter. Prof. Ward's theory is to my mind the most important that has been offered the world since the Theory of Evolution; and without exception the most important that has ever been put forward concerning women.

Among the many paradoxes which we find in human life is our low average standard of health and beauty, compared with our power and knowledge. All creatures suffer from conflict with the elements; from enemies without and within—the prowling devourers of the forest, and "the terror that walketh in darkness" and attacks the body from inside, in hidden millions.

Among wild animals generally, there is a certain standard of excellence; if you shoot a bear or a bird, it is a fair sample of the species; you do not say, "O what an ugly one!" or "This must have been an invalid!"

Where we have domesticated any animal, and interfered with its natural habits, illness has followed; the dog is said to have the most diseases second to man; the horse comes next; but the wild ones put us to shame by their superior health and the beauty that belongs to right development.

In our long ages of blind infancy we assume that sickness was a visitation frown the gods; some still believe this, holding it to be a special prerogative of divinity to afflict us in this way. We speak of "the ills that flesh is heir to" as if the inheritance was entailed and inalienable. Only of late years, after much study and long struggle with this old belief which made us submit to sickness as a blow from the hand of God, we are beginning to learn something of the many causes of our many diseases, and how to remove some of them.

It is still true, however, that almost every one of us is to some degree abnormal; the features asymmetrical, the vision defective, the digestion unreliable, the nervous system erratic—we are but a job lot even in what we call "good health"; and are subject to a burden of pain and premature death that would make life hideous if it were not so ridiculously unnecessary.

As to beauty—we do not think of expecting it save in the rarely exceptional case. Look at the faces—the figures—in any crowd you meet; compare the average man or the average woman with the normal type of human beauty as given us in picture and statue; and consider if there is not some general cause for so general a condition of ugliness.

Moreover, leaving our defective bodies concealed by garments; what are those garments, as conducive to health and beauty? Is the practical ugliness of our men's attire, and the impractical absurdity of our women's, any contribution to human beauty? Look at our houses—are they beautiful? Even the houses of the rich?

We do not even know that we ought to live in a world of overflowing loveliness; and that our contribution to it should be the loveliest of all. We are so sodden in the dull ugliness of our interiors, so used to calling a tame weary low-toned color scheme "good taste," that only children dare frankly yearn for Beauty—and they are speedily educated out of it.

The reasons specially given for our low standards of health and beauty are ignorance, poverty, and the evil effects of special trades. The Man with the Hoe becomes brother to the ox because of over-much hoeing; the housepainter is lead-poisoned because of his painting; books have been written to show the injurious influence of nearly all our industries upon workers.

These causes are sound as far as they go; but do not cover the whole ground.

The farmer may be muscle-bound and stooping from his labor; but that does not account for his dyspepsia or his rheumatism.

Then we allege poverty as covering all. Poverty does cover a good deal. But when we find even a half-fed savage better developed than a well paid cashier; and a poor peasant woman a more vigorous mother than the idle wife of a rich man, poverty is not enough.

Then we say ignorance explains it. But there are most learned professors who are ugly and asthmathic; there are even doctors who can boast no beauty and but moderate health; there are some of the petted children of the wealthy, upon whom every care is lavished from birth, and who still are ill to look at and worse to marry.

All these special causes are admitted, given their due share in lowering our standards, but there is another far more universal in its application and its effects. Let us look back on our little ancestors the beasts, and see what keeps them so true to type.

The type itself set by that balance of conditions and forces we call "natural selection." As the environment changes they must be adapted to it, if they cannot so adapt themselves they die. Those who live are, by living, proven capable of maintaining themselves. Every creature which has remained on earth, while so many less effective kinds died out, remains as a conqueror. The speed of the deer—the constant use of speed—is what keeps it alive and makes it healthy and beautiful. The varied activities of the life of a leopard are what have developed the sinuous gracile strength we so admire. It is what the creature does for its living, its daily life-long exercise which makes it what it is.

But there is another great natural force which works steadily to keep all animals up to the race standard; that is sexual selection. Throughout nature the male is the variant, as we have already noted. His energy finds vent not only in that profuse output of decorative appendages Ward defines as "masculine efflorescence" but in variations not decorative, not useful or desirable at all.

The female, on the other hand, varies much less, remaining nearer the race type; and her function is to select among these varying males the specimens most valuable to the race. In the intense masculine competition the victor must necessarily be stronger than his fellows; he is first proven equal to his environment by having lived to grow up, then more than equal to his fellows by overcoming them. This higher grade of selection also develops not only the characteristics necessary to make a living; but secondary ones, often of a purely aesthetic nature, which make much of what we call beauty. Between the two, all who live must be up to a certain grade, and those who become parents must be above it; a masterly arrangement surely!

Here is where, during the period of our human history, we in our newborn consciousness and imperfect knowledge, have grievously interfered with the laws of nature. The ancient proprietary family, treating the woman as a slave, keeping her a prisoner and subject to the will of her master, cut her off at once from the exercise of those activities which alone develop and maintain the race type.

Take the one simple quality of speed. We are a creature built for speed, a free swift graceful animal; and among savages this is still seen—the capacity for running, mile after mile, hour after hour. Running is as natural a gait for *genus homo* as for *genus cervus.* Now suppose among deer, the doe was prohibited from running; the stag continuing free on the mountain; the doe living in caves and pens, unequal to any exercise. The effect on the species would be, inevitably, to reduce its speed.

In this way, by keeping women to one small range of duties, and in most cases housebound, we have interfered with natural selection and its resultant health and beauty. It can easily be seen what the effect on the race would have been if all men had been veiled and swathed, hidden in harems, kept to the tent or house, and confined to the activities of a house-servant. Our stalwart laborers, our proud soldiers, our athletes, would never have appeared under such circumstances. The confinement to the house alone, cutting women off from sunshine and air, is by itself an injury; and the range of occupation allowed them is not such as to develop a high standard of either health or beauty. Thus we have cut off half the race from the strengthening influence of natural selection, and so lowered our race-standards in large degree.

This alone, however, would not have hid such mischievous effects but for our further blunder in completely reversing nature's order of sexual selection. It is quite possible that even under confinement and restriction women could have kept up the race level, passably, through this great function of selection; but here is the great fundamental error of the Androcentric Culture. Assuming to be the possessor of women, their owner and master, able at will to give, buy and sell, or do with as he pleases, man became the selector.

It seems a simple change; and in those early days, wholly ignorant of natural laws, there was no suspicion that any mischief would result. In the light of modern knowledge, however, the case is clear. The woman was deprived of the beneficent action of natural selection, and the man was then, by his own act, freed from the stern but elevating effect of sexual selection. Nothing was required of the woman by natural selection save such capacity as should please her master; nothing was required of the man by sexual selection save power to take by force, or buy, a woman.

It does not take a very high standard of feminine intelligence, strength, skill, health, or beauty to be a houseservant, or even a housekeeper; witness the average.

It does not take a very high standard of masculine, intelligence, strength, skill, health or beauty to maintain a woman in that capacity—witness average.

Here at the very root of our physiological process, at the beginning of life, we have perverted the order of nature, and are suffering the consequences.

It has been held by some that man as the selector has developed beauty, more beauty than we had before; and we point to the charms of our women as compared with those of the squaw. The answer to this is that the squaw belongs to a decadent race; that she too is subject to the man, that the comparison to have weight should be made between our women and the women of the matriarchate—an obvious impossibility. We have not on earth women in a state of normal freedom and full development; but we have enough difference in their placing to learn that human strength and beauty grows with woman's freedom and activity.

The second answer is that much of what man calls beauty in woman is not human beauty at all, but gross overdevelopment of certain points which appeal to him as a male. The excessive fatness, previously referred to, is a case in point; that being considered beauty in a woman which is in reality an element of weakness, inefficiency and ill-health. The relatively small size of women, deliberately preferred, steadfastly chosen, and so built into the race, is a blow at real human progress in every particular. In our upward journey we should and do grow larger, leaving far behind us our dwarfish progenitors. Yet the male, in his unnatural position as selector, preferring for reasons both practical and sentimental, to have "his woman" smaller than himself, has deliberately striven to lower the standard of size in the race. We used to read in the novels of the last generation, "He was a magnificent specimen of manhood"—"Her golden head reached scarcely to his shoulder"—"She was a fairy creature—the tiniest of her sex." Thus we have mated, and yet expected that by some hocus pocus the boys would all "take after their father," and the girls, their mother. In his efforts to improve the breed of other animals, man has never tried to deliberately cross the large and small and expect to keep up the standard of size.

As a male he is appealed to by the ultra-feminine, and has given small thought to effects on the race. He was not designed to do the selecting. Under his fostering care we have bred a race of women who are physically weak enough to be handed about like invalids; or mentally weak enough to pretend they are—and to like it. We have made women who respond so perfectly to the force which made them, that they attach all their idea of beauty to those characteristics which attract men; sometimes humanly ugly without even knowing it.

For instance, our long restriction to house-limits, the heavy limitations of our clothing, and the heavier ones of traditional decorum, have made women disproportionately short-legged. This is a particularly undignified and injurious characteristic, bred in women and inherited by men, most seen among those races which keep their women most closely. Yet when one woman escapes the tendency and appears with a normal length of femur and tibia, a normal height of hip and shoulder, she is criticized and called awkward by her squatty sisters!

The most convenient proof of the inferiority of women in human beauty is shown by those composite statues prepared by Mr. Sargent for the World's Fair of '93. These were made from gymnasium measurements of thousands of young collegians of both sexes all over America. The statue of the girl has a pretty face, small hands and feet, rather nice arms, though weak; but the legs are too thick and short; the chest and shoulders poor; and the trunk is quite pitiful in its weakness. The figure of the man is much better proportioned.

Thus the effect on human beauty of masculine selection.

Beyond this positive deteriorative effect on women through man's arbitrary choice comes the negative effect of woman's lack of choice. Bought or stolen or given by her father, she was deprived of the innately feminine right and duty of choosing. "Who giveth this woman?" we still inquire in our archaic marriage service, and one man steps forward and gives her to another man.

Free, the female chose the victor, and the vanquished went unmated—and without progeny. Dependent, having to be fed and cared for by some man, the victors take their pick perhaps, but the vanquished take what is left; and the poor women, "marrying for a home," take anything. As a consequence the inferior male is as free to transmit his inferiority as the superior to give better qualities, and does so—beyond computation. In modern days, women are freer, in some countries freer than in others; here in modern America freest of all; and the result is seen in our improving standards of health and beauty.

Still there remains the field of inter-masculine competition, does there not? Do not the males still struggle together? Is not that as of old, a source of race advantage?

To some degree it is. When life was simple and our activities consisted mainly in fighting and hard work; the male who could vanquish the others was bigger and stronger. But inter-masculine competition ceases to be of such advantage when we enter the field of social service. What is required in organized society is the specialization of the individual, the development of special talents, not always of immediate benefit to the man himself, but of ultimate benefit to society. The best social servant, progressive, meeting future needs, is almost always at a disadvantage besides the well-established lower types. We need, for social service, qualities quite different from the simple masculine characteristics—desire, combat, self-expression.

By keeping what we call "the outside world" so wholly male, we keep up masculine standards at the expense of human ones. This may be broadly seen in the slow and painful development of industry and science as compared to the easy dominance of warfare throughout all history until our own times.

The effect of all this ultra masculine competition upon health and beauty is but too plainly to be seen. Among men the male idea of what is good looking is accentuated beyond reason. Read about any "hero" you please; or study the products of the illustrator and note the broad shoulders, the rugged features, the strong, square, determined jaw. That jaw is in evidence if everything else fails. He may be cross-eyed, wide-eared, thick-necked, bandy-legged—what you please; but he must have a more or less prognathous jaw.

Meanwhile any anthropologist will show you that the line of human development is away from that feature of the bulldog and the alligator, and toward the measured dignity of the Greek type. The possessor of that kind of jaw may enable male to conquer male, but does not make him of any more service to society; of any better health or higher beauty.

Further, in the external decoration of our bodies, what is the influence here of masculine dominance.

We have before spoken of the peculiar position of our race in that the woman is the only female creature who carries the burden of sex ornament. This amazing reversal of the order of nature results at its mildest in a perversion of the natural feminine instincts of love and service, and an appearance of the masculine instincts of self-expression and display. Alone among all female things do women decorate and preen themselves and exhibit their borrowed plumage (literally!) to attract the favor of the male. This ignominy is forced upon them by their position of economic dependence; and their general helplessness. As all broader life is made to depend, for them, on whom they marry, indeed as even the necessities of life so often depend on their marrying someone, they have been driven into this form of competition, so alien to the true female attitude.

The result is enough to make angels weep—and laugh. Perhaps no step in the evolution of beauty went farther than our human power of making a continuous fabric; soft and mobile, showing any color and texture desired. The beauty of the human body is supreme, and when we add to it the flow of color, the ripple of fluent motion, that comes of a soft, light garment over free limbs—it is a new field of loveliness and delight. Naturally this should have filled the whole world with a new pleasure. Our garments, first under right natural selection developing perfect use, under right sex selection developing beauty; and further, as our human aesthetic sense progresses, showing a noble symbolism, would have been an added strength and glory, a ceaseless joy.

What is the case?

Men, under a too strictly inter-masculine environment, have evolved the mainly useful but beautiless costume common to-day; and women—?

Women wear beautiful garments when they happen to be the fashion; and ugly garments when they are the fashion, and show no signs of knowing the difference. They show no added pride in the beautiful, no hint of mortification in the hideous, and are not even sensitive under criticism, or open to any persuasion or argument. Why should they be?

Their condition, physical and mental, is largely abnormal, their whole passionate absorption in dress and decoration is abnormal, and they have never looked, from a frankly human standpoint, at their position and its peculiarities, until the present age.

In the effect of our wrong relation on the world's health, we have spoken of the check to vigor and growth due to the housebound state of women and their burdensome clothes. There follow other influences, similar in origin, even more evil in result. To roughly and briefly classify we may distinguish the diseases due to bad air, to bad food, and that field of cruel mischief we are only now beginning to discuss—the diseases directly due to the erroneous relation between men and women.

We are the only race where the female depends on the male for a livelihood. We are the only race that practices prostitution. From the first harmless-looking but abnormal general relation follows the well recognized evil of the second, so long called "a social necessity," and from it, in deadly sequence, comes the "wages of sin;" death not only of the guilty, but of the innocent. It is no light part of our criticism of the Androcentric Culture that a society based on masculine desires alone, has willingly sacrificed such an army of women; and has repaid the sacrifice by the heaviest punishments.

That the unfortunate woman should sicken and die was held to be her just punishment; that man too should bear part penalty was found unavoidable, though much legislation and medical effort has been spent to shield him; but to the further consequences society is but now waking up.

IV

Men and Art

Among the many counts in which women have been proven inferior to men in human development is the oft-heard charge that there are no great women artists. Where one or two are proudly exhibited in evidence, they are either pooh-poohed as not very great, or held to be the trifling exceptions which do but prove the rule.

Defenders of women generally make the mistake of over-estimating their performances, instead of accepting, and explaining, the visible facts. What are the facts as to the relation of men and women to art? And what, in especial, has been the effect upon art of a solely masculine expression?

When we look for the beginnings of art, we find ourselves in a period of crude decoration of the person and of personal belongings. Tattooing, for instance, is an early form of decorative art, still in practice among certain classes, even in advanced people. Most boys, if they are in contact with this early art, admire it, and wish to adorn themselves therewith; some do so—to later mortification. Early personal decoration consisted largely in direct mutilation of the body, and the hanging upon it, or fastening to it, of decorative objects. This we see among savages still, in its gross and primitive forms monopolized by men, then shared by women, and, in our time, left almost wholly to them. In personal decoration today, women are still near the savage. The "artists" developed in this field of art are the tonsorial, the sartorial, and all those specialized adorners of the body commonly known as "beauty doctors."

Here, as in other cases, the greatest artists are men. The greatest milliners, the greatest dressmakers and tailors, the greatest hairdressers, and the masters and designers in all our decorative toilettes and accessories, are men. Women, in this as in so many other lines, consume rather than produce. They carry the major part of personal decoration today; but the decorator is the man. In the decoration of objects, woman, as the originator of primitive industry, originated also the primitive arts; and in the pottery, basketry, leatherwork, needlework, weaving, with all beadwork, dyeing and embroideries of ancient peoples we see the work of the woman decorator. Much of this is strong and beautiful, but its time is long past. The art which is part of industry, natural, simple, spontaneous, making beauty in every object of use, adding pleasure to labor and to life, is not Art with a large A, the Art which requires Artists, among whom are so few women of note.

Art as a profession, and the Artist as a professional, came later; and by that time women had left the freedom and power of the matriarchate and become slaves in varying degree. The women who were idle pets in harems, or the women who worked hard as servants, were alike cut off from the joy of making things. Where constructive work remained to them, art remained, in its early decorative form. Men, in the proprietary family, restricting the natural industry of women to personal service, cut off their art with their industry, and by so much impoverished the world.

There is no more conspicuously pathetic proof of the aborted development of women than this commonplace—their lack of a civilized art sense. Not only in the childish and savage display upon their bodies, but in the pitiful products they hang upon the walls of the home, is seen the arrest in normal growth.

After ages of culture, in which men have developed Architecture, Sculpture, Painting, Music and the Drama, we find women in their primitive environment making flowers of wax, and hair, and worsted; doing mottoes of perforated cardboard, making crazy quilts and mats and "tidies"—as if they lived in a long past age, or belonged to a lower race.

This, as part of the general injury to women dating from the beginning of our androcentric culture, reacts heavily upon the world at large. Men, specializing, giving their lives to the continuous pursuit of one line of service, have lifted our standard in aesthetic culture, as they have in other matters; but by refusing the same growth to women, they have not only weakened and reduced the output, but ruined the market as it were, hopelessly and permanently kept down the level of taste.

Among the many sides of this great question, some so terrible, some so pathetic, some so utterly absurd, this particular phase of life is especially easy to study and understand, and has its own elements of amusement. Men, holding women at the level of domestic service, going on themselves to lonely heights of achievement, have found their efforts hampered and their attainments rendered barren and unsatisfactory by the amazing indifference of the world at large. As the world at large consists half of women, and wholly of their children, it would seem patent to the meanest understanding that the women must be allowed to rise in order to lift the world. But such has not been the method—heretofore.

We have spoken so far in this chapter of the effect of men on art through their interference with the art of women. There are other sides to the question. Let us consider once more the essential characteristics of maleness, and see how they have affected art, keeping always in mind the triune distinction between masculine, feminine and human. Perhaps we shall best see this difference by considering what the development of art might have been on purely human terms.

The human creature, as such, naturally delights in construction, and adds decoration to construction as naturally. The cook, making little regular patterns around the edge of the pie, does so from a purely human instinct, the innate eye-pleasure in regularity, symmetry, repetition, and alternation. Had this natural social instinct grown unchecked in us, it would have manifested itself in a certain proportion of specialists—artists of all sorts—and an accompanying development of appreciation on the part of the rest of us. Such is the case in primitive art; the maker of beauty is upheld and rewarded by a popular appreciation of her work—or his.

Had this condition remained, we should find a general level of artistic expression and appreciation far higher than we see now. Take the one field of textile art, for instance: that wide and fluent medium of expression, the making of varied fabrics, the fashioning of garments and the decoration of them—all this is human work and human pleasure. It should have led us to a condition where every human being was a pleasure to the eye, appropriately and beautifully clothed.

Our real condition in this field is too patent to need emphasis; the stiff, black ugliness of our men's attire; the irritating variegated folly of our women's; the way in which we spoil the beauty and shame the dignity of childhood by modes of dress.

In normal human growth, our houses would be a pleasure to the eye; our furniture and utensils, all our social products, would blossom into beauty as naturally as they still do in those low stages of social evolution where our major errors have not yet borne full fruit.

Applied art in all its forms is a human function, common to every one to some degree, either in production or appreciation, or both. "Pure art," as an ideal, is also human; and the single-hearted devotion of the true artist to this ideal is one of the highest forms of the social sacrifice. Of all the thousand ways by which humanity is specialized for inter-service, none is more exquisite than this; the evolution of the social Eye, or Ear, or Voice, the development of those whose work is wholly for others, and to whom the appreciation of others is as the bread of life. This we should have in a properly developed community; the pleasure of applied art in the making and using of everything we have; and then the high joy of the Great Artist, and the noble work thereof, spread far and wide.

What do we find?

Applied art at a very low level; small joy either for the maker or the user. Pure art, a fine-spun specialty, a process carried on by an elect few who openly despise the unappreciative many. Art has become an occult profession requiring a long special education even to enjoy, and evolving a jargon of criticism which becomes more esoteric yearly.

Let us now see what part in this undesirable outcome is due to our Androcentric Culture.

As soon as the male of our species assumed the exclusive right to perform all social functions, he necessarily brought to that performance the advantages—and disadvantages—of maleness, of those dominant characteristics, desire, combat, self-expression.

Desire has overweighted art in many visible forms; it is prominent in painting and music, almost monopolizes fiction, and has pitifully degraded dancing.

Combat is not so easily expressed in art, where even competition is on a high plane; but the last element is the main evil, self-expression. This impulse is inherently and ineradicably masculine. It rests on that most basic of distinctions between the sexes, the centripetal and centrifugal forces of the universe. In the very nature of the sperm-cell and the germ-cell we find this difference: the one attracts, gathers, draws in; the other repels, scatters, pushes out. That projective impulse is seen in the male nature everywhere; the constant urge toward expression, to all boasting and display. This spirit, like all things masculine, is perfectly right and admirable in its place.

It is the duty of the male, as a male, to vary; bursting forth in a thousand changing modifications—the female, selecting, may so incorporate beneficial changes in the race. It is his duty to thus express himself—an essentially masculine duty; but masculinity is one thing, and art is another. Neither the masculine nor the feminine has any place in art—Art is Human.

It is not in any faintest degree allied to the personal processes of reproduction; but is a social process, a most distinctive social process, quite above the plane of sex. The true artist transcends his sex, or her sex. If this is not the case, the art suffers.

Dancing is an early, and a beautiful art; direct expression of emotion through the body; beginning in subhuman type, among male birds, as the bower-bird of New Guinea, and the dancing crane, who swing and caper before their mates. Among early peoples we find it a common form of social expression in tribal dances of all sorts, religious, military, and other. Later it becomes a more explicit form of celebration, as among the Greeks; in whose exquisite personal culture dancing and music held high place.

But under the progressive effects of purely masculine dominance we find the broader human elements of dancing left out, and the sex-element more and more emphasized. As practiced by men alone dancing has become a mere display of physical agility, a form of exhibition common to all males. As practiced by men and women together we have our social dances, so lacking in all the varied beauty of posture and expression, so steadily becoming a pleasant form of dalliance.

As practiced by women alone we have one of the clearest proofs of the degrading effect of masculine dominance:—the dancing girl. In the frank sensualism of the Orient, this personage is admired and enjoyed on her merits. We, more sophisticated in this matter, joke shamefacedly about "the bald-headed row," and occasionally burst forth in shrill scandal over some dinner party where ladies clad in a veil and a bracelet dance on the table. Nowhere else in the whole range of life on earth, is this degradation found—the female capering and prancing before the male. It is absolutely and essentially his function, not hers. That we, as a race, present this pitiful spectacle, a natural art wrested to unnatural ends, a noble art degraded to ignoble ends, has one clear cause.

Architecture, in its own nature, is least affected by that same cause. The human needs secured by it, are so human, so unescapably human, that we find less trace of excessive masculinity than in other arts. It meets our social demands, it expresses in lasting form our social feeling, up to the highest; and it has been injured not so much by an excess of masculinity as by a lack of femininity.

The most universal architectural expression is in the home; the home is essentially a place for the woman and the child; yet the needs of woman and child are not expressed in our domestic architecture. The home is built on lines of ancient precedent, mainly as an industrial form; the kitchen is its working centre rather than the nursery.

Each man wishes his home to preserve and seclude his woman, his little harem of one; and in it she is to labor for his comfort or to manifest his ability to maintain her in idleness. The house is the physical expression of the limitations of women; and as such it fills the world with a small drab ugliness. A dwelling house is rarely a beautiful object. In order to be such, it should truly express simple and natural relations; or grow in larger beauty as our lives develop.

The deadlock for architectural progress, the low level of our general taste, the everlasting predominance of the commonplace in buildings, is the natural result of the proprietary family and its expression in this form.

In sculpture we have a noble art forcing itself into some service through many limitations. Its check, as far as it comes under this line of study, has been indicated in our last chapter; the degradation of the human body, the vicious standards of sex-consciousness enforced under the name of modesty, the covered ugliness, which we do not recognize, all this is a deadly injury to free high work in sculpture.

With a nobly equal womanhood, stalwart and athletic; with the high standards of beauty and of decorum which we can never have without free womanhood; we should show a different product in this great art.

An interesting note in passing is this: when we seek to express socially our noblest, ideas, Truth; Justice; Liberty; we use the woman's body as the highest human type. But in doing this, the artist, true to humanity and not biassed by sex, gives us a strong, grand figure, beautiful indeed, but never *decorated*. Fancy Liberty in ruffles and frills, with rings in her ears—or nose.

Music is injured by a one-sided handling, partly in the excess of the one dominant masculine passion, partly by the general presence of egoism; that tendency to self-expression instead of social expression, which so disfigures our art; and this is true also of poetry.

Miles and miles of poetry consist of the ceaseless outcry of the male for the female, which is by no means so overwhelming as a feature of human life as he imagines it; and other miles express his other feelings, with that ingenuous lack of reticence which is at its base essentially masculine. Having a pain, the poet must needs pour it forth, that his woe be shared and sympathized with.

As more and more women writers flock into the field there is room for fine historic study of the difference in sex feeling, and the gradual emergence of the human note.

Literature, and in especial the art of fiction, is so large a field for this study that it will have a chapter to itself; this one but touching on these various forms; and indicating lines of observation.

That best known form of art which to my mind needs no qualifying description—painting—is also a wide field; and cannot be done full justice to within these limits. The effect upon it of too much masculinity is not so much in choice of subject as in method and spirit. The artist sees beauty of form and color where the ordinary observer does not; and paints the old and ugly with as much enthusiasm as the young and beautiful—sometimes. If there is in some an over-emphasis of feminine attractions it is counterbalanced in others by a far broader line of work.

But the main evils of a too masculine art lie in the emphasis laid on self-expression. The artist, passionately conscious of how he feels, strives to make other people aware of these sensations. This is now so generally accepted by critics, so seriously advanced by painters, that what is called "the art world" accepts it as established.

If a man paints the sea, it is not to make you see and feel as a sight of that same ocean would, but to make you see and feel how he, personally, was affected by it; a matter surely of the narrowest importance. The ultra-masculine artist, extremely sensitive, necessarily, and full of the natural urge to expression of the sex, uses the medium of art as ingenuously as the partridge-cock uses his wings in drumming on the log; or the bull moose stamps and bellows; not narrowly as a mate call, but as a form of expression of his personal sensations.

The higher the artist the more human he is, the broader his vision, the more he sees for humanity, and expresses for humanity, and the less personal, the less ultra-masculine, is his expression.

V

MASCULINE LITERATURE

When we are offered a "woman's" paper, page, or column, we find it filled with matter supposed to appeal to women as a sex or class; the writer mainly dwelling upon the Kaiser's four K's—Kuchen, Kinder, Kirche, Kleider. They iterate and reiterate endlessly the discussion of cookery, old and new; of the care of children; of the overwhelming subject of clothing; and of moral instruction. All this is recognized as "feminine" literature, and it must have some appeal else the women would not read it. What parallel have we in "masculine" literature?

"None!" is the proud reply. "Men are people! Women, being 'the sex,' have their limited feminine interests, their feminine point of view, which must be provided for. Men, however, are not restricted—to them belongs the world's literature!"

Yes, it has belonged to them—ever since there was any. They have written it and they have read it. It is only lately that women, generally speaking, have been taught to read; still more lately that they have been allowed to write. It is but a little while since Harriet Martineau concealed her writing beneath her sewing when visitors came in—writing was "masculine"—sewing "feminine."

We have not, it Is true, confined men to a narrowly construed "masculine sphere," and composed a special literature suited to it. Their effect on literature has been far wider than that, monopolizing this form of art with special favor. It was suited above all others to the dominant impulse of self-expression; and being, as we have seen essentially and continually "the sex;" they have impressed that sex upon this art overwhelmingly; they have given the world a masculized literature.

It is hard for us to realize this. We can readily see, that if women had always written the books, no men either writing or reading them, that would have surely "feminized" our literature; but we have not in our minds the concept, much less the word, for an overmasculized influence.

Men having been accepted as humanity, women but a side-issue; (most literally if we accept the Hebrew legend!), whatever men did or said was human—and not to be criticized. In no department of life is it easier to contravert this old belief; to show how the male sex as such differs from the human type; and how this maleness has monopolized and disfigured a great social function.

Human life is a very large affair; and literature is its chief art. We live, humanly, only through our power of communication. Speech gives us this power laterally, as it were, in immediate personal contact. For permanent use speech becomes oral tradition—a poor dependence. Literature gives not only an infinite multiplication to the lateral spread of communion but adds the vertical reach. Through it we know the past, govern the present, and influence the future. In its servicable common forms it is the indispensable daily servant of our lives; in its nobler flights as a great art no means of human inter-change goes so far.

In these brief limits we can touch but lightly on some phases of so great a subject; and will rest the case mainly on the effect of an exclusively masculine handling of the two fields of history and fiction. In poetry and the drama the same influence is easily traced, but in the first two it is so baldly prominent as to defy objection.

History is, or should be, the story of our racial life. What have men made it? The story of warfare and conquest. Begin at the very beginning with the carven stones of Egypt, the clay records of Chaldea, what do we find of history?

"I Pharaoh, King of Kings! Lord of Lords! (etc. etc.), went down into the miserable land of Kush, and slew of the inhabitants thereof an hundred and forty and two thousands!" That, or something like it, is the kind of record early history gives us.

The story of Conquering Kings, who and how many they killed and enslaved; the grovelling adulation of the abased; the unlimited jubilation of the victor; from the primitive state of most ancient kings, and the Roman triumphs where queens walked in chains, down to our omni present soldier's monuments: the story of war and conquest— war and conquest—over and over; with such boasting and triumph, such cock-crow and flapping of wings as show most unmistakably the natural source.

All this will strike the reader at first as biased and unfair. "That was the way people lived in those days!" says the reader.

No—it was not the way women lived.

"O, women!" says the reader, "Of course not! Women are different."

Yea, women are different; and *men are different!* Both of them, as sexes, differ from the human norm, which is social life and all social development. Society was slowly growing in all those black blind years.

The arts, the sciences, the trades and crafts and professions, religion, philosophy, government, law, commerce, agriculture—all the human processes were going on as well as they were able, between wars.

The male naturally fights, and naturally crows, triumphs over his rival and takes the prize—therefore was he made male. Maleness means war.

Not only so; but being male, he cares only for male interests. Men, being the sole arbiters of what should be done and said and written, have given us not only a social growth scarred and thwarted from the beginning by continual destruction; but a history which is one unbroken record of courage and red cruelty, of triumph and black shame.

As to what went on that was of real consequence, the great slow steps of the working world, the discoveries and inventions, the real progress of humanity—that was not worth recording, from a masculine point of view. Within this last century, "the woman's century," the century of the great awakening, the rising demand for freedom, political, economic, and domestic, we are beginning to write real history, human history, and not merely masculine history. But that great branch of literature—Hebrew, Greek, Roman, and all down later times, shows beyond all question, the influence of our androcentric culture.

Literature is the most powerful and necessary of the arts, and fiction is its broadest form. If art "holds the mirror up to nature" this art's mirror is the largest of all, the most used. Since our very life depends on some communication; and our progress is in proportion to our fullness and freedom of communication; since real communication requires mutual understanding; so in the growth of the social consciousness, we note from the beginning a passionate interest in other people's lives.

The art which gives humanity consciousness is the most vital art. Our greatest dramatists are lauded for their breadth of knowledge of "human nature," their range of emotion and understanding; our greatest poets are those who most deeply and widely experience and reveal the feelings of the human heart; and the power of fiction is that it can reach and express this great field of human life with no limits but those of the author.

When fiction began it was the legitimate child of oral tradition; a product of natural brain activity; the legend constructed instead of remembered. (This stage is with us yet as seen in the constant changes in repetition of popular jokes and stories.)

Fiction to-day has a much wider range; yet it is still restricted, heavily and most mischievously restricted.

What is the preferred subject matter of fiction?

There are two main branches found everywhere, from the Romaunt of the Rose to the Purplish Magazine;—the Story of Adventure, and the Love Story.

The Story-of-Adventure branch is not so thick as the other by any means, but it is a sturdy bough for all that. Stevenson and Kipling have proved its immense popularity, with the whole brood of detective stories and the tales of successful rascality we call "picaresque" Our most popular weekly shows the broad appeal of this class of fiction.

All these tales of adventure, of struggle and difficulty; of hunting and fishing and fighting; of robbing and murdering, catching and punishing, are distinctly and essentially masculine. They do not touch on human processes, social processes, but on the special field of predatory excitement so long the sole province of men.

It is to be noted here that even in the overwhelming rise of industrial interests to-day, these, when used as the basis for a story, are forced into line with one, or both, of these two main branches of fiction;—conflict or love. Unless the story has one of these "interests" in it, there is no story— so holds the editor; the dictum being, put plainly, "life has no interests except conflict and love!"

It is surely something more than a coincidence that these are the two essential features of masculinity—Desire and Combat—Love and War.

As a matter of fact the major interests of life are in line with its major processes; and these—in our stage of human development—are more varied than our fiction would have us believe. Half the world consists of women, we should remember, who are types of human life as well as men, and their major processes are not those of conflict and adventure, their love means more than mating. Even on so poor a line of distinction as the "woman's column" offers, if women are to be kept to their four Ks, there should be a "men's column" also; and all the "sporting news" and fish stories be put in that; they are not world interests; they are male interests.

Now for the main branch—the Love Story. Ninety per cent. of fiction is In this line; this is preeminently the major interest of life— given in fiction. What is the love-story, as rendered by this art?

It is the story of the pre-marital struggle. It is the Adventures of Him in Pursuit of Her—and it stops when he gets her! Story after story, age after age, over and over and over, this ceaseless repetition of the Preliminaries.

Here is Human Life. In its large sense, its real sense, it is a matter of inter-relation between individuals and groups, covering all emotions, all processes, all experiences. Out of this vast field of human life fiction arbitrarily selects one emotion, one process, one experience, as its necessary base.

"Ah! but we are persons most of all!" protests the reader. "This is personal experience—it has the universal appeal!"

Take human life personally then. Here is a Human Being, a life, covering some seventy years; involving the changing growth of many faculties; the ever new marvels of youth, the long working time of middle life, the slow ripening of age. Here is the human soul, in the human body, Living. Out of this field of personal life, with all of its emotions, processes, and experiences, fiction arbitrarily selects one emotion, one process, one experience, mainly of one sex.

The "love" of our stories is man's love of woman. If any dare dispute this, and say it treats equally of woman's love for man, I answer, "Then why do the stories stop at marriage?"

There is a current jest, revealing much, to this effect:

The young wife complains that the husband does not wait upon and woo her as he did before marriage; to which he replies, "Why should I run after the street-car when I've caught it?"

Woman's love for man, as currently treated in fiction is largely a reflex; it is the way he wants her to feel, expects her to feel; not a fair representation of how she does feel. If "love" is to be selected as the most important thing in life to write about, then the mother's love should be the principal subject: This is the main stream. This is the general underlying, world-lifting force. The "life-force," now so glibly chattered about, finds its fullest expression in motherhood; not in the emotions of an assistant in the preliminary stages.

What has literature, what has fiction, to offer concerning mother-love, or even concerning father-love, as compared to this vast volume of excitement about lover-love? Why is the search-light continually focussed upon a two or three years space of life "mid the blank miles round about?" Why indeed, except for the clear reason, that on a starkly masculine basis this is his one period of overwhelming interest and excitement.

If the beehive produced literature, the bee's fiction would be rich and broad; full of the complex tasks of comb-building and filling; the care and feeding of the young, the guardian-service of the queen;

and far beyond that it would spread to the blue glory of the summer sky, the fresh winds, the endless beauty and sweetness of a thousand thousand flowers. It would treat of the vast fecundity of motherhood, the educative and selective processes of the group-mothers; and the passion of loyalty, of social service, which holds the hive together.

But if the drones wrote fiction, it would have no subject matter save the feasting of many; and the nuptial flight, of one.

To the male, as such, this mating instinct is frankly the major interest of life; even the belligerent instincts are second to it. To the female, as such, it is for all its intensity, but a passing interest. In nature's economy, his is but a temporary devotion, hers the slow processes of life's fulfillment.

In Humanity we have long since, not outgrown, but overgrown, this stage of feeling. In Human Parentage even the mother's share begins to pale beside that ever-growing Social love and care, which guards and guides the children of to-day.

The art of literature in this main form of fiction is far too great a thing to be wholly governed by one dominant note. As life widened and intensified, the artist, if great enough, has transcended sex; and in the mightier works of the real masters, we find fiction treating of life, life in general, in all its complex relationships, and refusing to be held longer to the rigid canons of an androcentric past.

This was the power of Balzac—he took in more than this one field. This was the universal appeal of Dickens; he wrote of people, all kinds of people, doing all kinds of things. As you recall with pleasure some preferred novel of this general favorite, you find yourself looking narrowly for the "love story" in it. It is there—for it is part of life; but it does not dominate the whole scene—any more than it does in life.

The thought of the world is made and handed out to us in the main. The makers of books are the makers of thoughts and feelings for people in general. Fiction is the most popular form in which this world-food is taken. If it were true, it would teach us life easily, swiftly, truly; teach not by preaching but by truly re-presenting; and we should grow up becoming acquainted with a far wider range of life in books than could even be ours in person. Then meeting life in reality we should be wise— and not be disappointed.

As it is, our great sea of fiction is steeped and dyed and flavored all one way. A young man faces life—the seventy year stretch, remember, and is given book upon book wherein one set of feelings is continually vocalized and overestimated. He reads forever of love, good love and bad love, natural and unnatural, legitimate and illegitimate; with the unavoidable inference that there is nothing else going on.

If he is a healthy young man he breaks loose from the whole thing, despises "love stories" and takes up life as he finds it. But what impression he does receive from fiction is a false one, and he suffers without knowing it from lack of the truer broader views of life it failed to give him.

A young woman faces life—the seventy year stretch remember; and is given the same books—with restrictions. Remember the remark of Rochefoucauld, "There are thirty good stories in the world and twenty-nine cannot be told to women." There is a certain broad field of literature so grossly androcentric that for very shame men have tried to keep it to themselves. But in a milder form, the spades all named teaspoons, or at the worst appearing as trowels—the young woman is given the same fiction. Love and love and love—from "first sight" to marriage. There it stops—just the fluttering ribbon of announcement, "and lived happily ever after."

Is that kind of fiction any sort of picture of a woman's life? Fiction, under our androcentric culture, has not given any true picture of woman's life, very little of human life, and a disproportioned section of man's life.

As we daily grow more human, both of us, this noble art is changing for the better so fast that a short lifetime can mark the growth. New fields are opening and new laborers are working in them. But it is no swift and easy matter to disabuse the race mind from attitudes and habits inculcated for a thousand years. What we have been fed upon so long we are well used to, what we are used to we like, what we like we think is good and proper.

The widening demand for broader, truer fiction is disputed by the slow racial mind: and opposed by the marketers of literature on grounds of visible self-interest, as well as lethargic conservatism.

It is difficult for men, heretofore the sole producers and consumers of literature; and for women, new to the field, and following masculine canons because all the canons were masculine; to stretch their minds to a recognition of the change which is even now upon us.

This one narrow field has been for so long overworked, our minds are so filled with heroes and heroes continually repeating the one-act play, that when a book like David Harum is offered the publisher refuses it repeatedly, and finally insists on a "heart interest" being injected by force.

Did anyone read David Harum for that heart interest? Does anyone remember that heart interest? Has humanity no interests but those of the heart?

Robert Ellesmere was a popular book—but not because of its heart interest.

Uncle Tom's Cabin appealed to the entire world, more widely than any work of fiction that was ever written; but if anybody fell in love and married in it they have been forgotten. There was plenty of love in that book, love of family, love of friends, love of master for servant and servant for master; love of mother for child; love of married people for each other; love of humanity and love of God.

It was extremely popular. Some say it was not literature. That opinion will live, like the name of Empedocles.

The art of fiction is being re-born in these days. Life is discovered to be longer, wider, deeper, richer, than these monotonous players of one June would have us believe.

The humanizing of woman of itself opens five distinctly fresh fields of fiction: First the position of the young woman who is called upon to give up her "career"—her humanness—for marriage, and who objects to it; second, the middle-aged woman who at last discovers that her discontent is social starvation—that it is not more love that she wants, but more business in life: Third the interrelation of women with women—a thing we could never write about before because we never had it before: except in harems and convents: Fourth the inter-action between mothers and children; this not the eternal "mother and child," wherein the child is always a baby, but the long drama of personal relationship; the love and hope, the patience and power, the lasting joy and triumph, the slow eating disappointment which must never be owned to a living soul—here are grounds for novels that a million mothers and many million children would eagerly read: Fifth the new attitude of the full-grown woman who faces the demands of love with the high standards of conscious motherhood.

There are other fields, broad and brilliantly promising, but this chapter is meant merely to show that our one-sided culture has, in this art, most disproportionately overestimated the dominant instincts of the male—Love and War—an offense against art and truth, and an injury to life.

VI

Games and Sports

One of the sharpest distinctions both between the essential characters and the artificial positions of men and women, is in the matter of games and sports. By far the greater proportion of them are essentially masculine, and as such alien to women; while from those which are humanly interesting, women have been largely debarred by their arbitrary restrictions.

The play instinct is common to girls and boys alike; and endures in some measure throughout life. As other young animals express their abounding energies in capricious activities similar to those followed in the business of living, so small children gambol, physically, like lambs and kids; and as the young of higher kinds of animals imitate in their play the more complex activities of their elders, so do children imitate whatever activities they see about them. In this field of playing there is no sex.

Similarly in adult life healthy and happy persons, men and women, naturally express surplus energy in various forms of sport. We have here one of the most distinctively human manifestations. The great accumulation of social energy, and the necessary limitations of one kind of work, leave a human being tired of one form of action, yet still uneasy for lack of full expression; and this social need has been met by our great safety valve of games and sports.

In a society of either sex, or in a society without sex, there would still be both pleasure and use in games; they are vitally essential to human life. In a society of two sexes, wherein one has dictated all the terms of life, and the other has been confined to an extremely limited fraction of human living, we may look to see this great field of enjoyment as disproportionately divided.

It is not only that we have reduced the play impulse in women by restricting them to one set of occupations, and overtaxing their energies with mother-work and housework combined; and not only that by our androcentric conventions we further restrict their amusements; but we begin in infancy, and forcibly differentiate their methods of play long before any natural distinction would appear.

Take that universal joy the doll, or puppet, as an instance. A small imitation of a large known object carries delight to the heart of a child of either sex. The worsted cat, the wooden horse, the little wagon, the tin soldier, the wax doll, the toy village, the "Noah's Ark," the omnipresent "Teddy Bear," any and every small model of a real thing is a delight to the young human being. Of all things the puppet is the most intimate, the little image of another human being to play with. The fancy of the child, making endless combinations with these visible types, plays as freely as a kitten in the leaves; or gravely carries out some observed forms of life, as the kitten imitates its mother's hunting.

So far all is natural and human.

Now see our attitude toward child's play—under a masculine culture. Regarding women only as a sex, and that sex as manifest from infancy, we make and buy for our little girls toys suitable to this view. Being females—which means mothers, we must needs provide them with babies before they cease to be babies themselves; and we expect their play to consist in an imitation of maternal cares. The doll, the puppet, which interests all children, we have rendered as an eternal baby; and we foist them upon our girl children by ceaseless millions.

The doll, as such, is dear to the little boy as well as the girl, but not as a baby. He likes his jumping-jack, his worsted Sambo, often a genuine rag-doll; but he is discouraged and ridiculed in this. We do not expect the little boy to manifest a father's love and care for an imitation child—but we do expect the little girl to show maternal feelings for her imitation baby. It has not yet occurred to us that this is monstrous.

Little children should not be expected to show, in painful precocity, feelings which ought never to be experienced till they come at the proper age. Our kittens play at cat-sports, little Tom and Tabby together; but little Tabby does not play she is a mother!

Beyond the continuous dolls and their continuous dressing, we provide for our little girls tea sets and kitchen sets, doll's houses, little work-boxes—the imitation tools of their narrow trades. For the boy there is a larger choice. We make for them not only the essentially masculine toys of combat—all the enginery of mimic war; but also the models of human things, like boats, railroads, wagons. For them, too, are the comprehensive toys of the centuries, the kite, the top, the ball. As the boy gets old enough to play the games that require skill, he enters the world-lists, and the little sister, left inside, with her everlasting dolls, learns that she is "only a girl," and "mustn't play with boys—boys are so rough!" She has her doll and her tea set. She "plays house." If very active she may jump rope, in solitary enthusiasm, or in combination of from two to four. Her brother is playing games. From this time on he plays the games of the world. The "sporting page" should be called "the Man's Page" as that array of recipes, fashions and cheap advice is called "the Woman's Page."

One of the immediate educational advantages of the boy's position is that he learns "team work." This is not a masculine characteristic, it is a human one; a social power. Women are equally capable of it by nature; but not by education. Tending one's imitation baby is not team-work; nor is playing house. The little girl is kept forever within the limitations of her mother's "sphere" of action; while the boy learns life, and fancies that his new growth is due to his superior sex.

Now there are certain essential distinctions in the sexes, which would manifest themselves to some degree even in normally reared children; as for instance the little male would be more given to fighting and destroying; the little female more to caring for and constructing things.

"Boys are so destructive!" we say with modest pride—as if it was in some way a credit to them. But early youth is not the time to display sex distinction; and they should be discouraged rather than approved.

The games of the world, now the games of men, easily fall into two broad classes—games of skill and games of chance.

The interest and pleasure in the latter is purely human, and as such is shared by the two sexes even now. Women, in the innocent beginnings or the vicious extremes of this line of amusement, make as wild gamblers as men. At the races, at the roulette wheel, at the bridge table, this is clearly seen.

In games of skill we have a different showing. Most of these are developed by and for men; but when they are allowed, women take part in them with interest and success. In card games, in chess, checkers, and the like, in croquet and tennis, they play, and play well if well-trained. Where they fall short in so many games, and are so wholly excluded in others, is not for lack of human capacity, but for lack of masculinity. Most games are male. In their element of desire to win, to get the prize, they are male; and in their universal attitude of competition they are male, the basic spirit of desire and of combat working out through subtle modern forms.

There is something inherently masculine also in the universal dominance of the projectile in their games. The ball is the one unescapable instrument of sport. From the snapped marble of infancy to the flying missile of the bat, this form endures. To send something forth with violence; to throw it, bat it, kick it, shoot it; this impulse seems to date back to one of the twin forces of the universe—the centrifugal and centripetal energies between which swing the planets.

The basic feminine impulse is to gather, to put together, to construct; the basic masculine impulse to scatter, to disseminate, to destroy. It seems to give pleasure to a man to bang something and drive it from him; the harder he hits it and the farther it goes the better pleased he is.

Games of this sort will never appeal to women. They are not wrong; not necessarily evil in their place; our mistake is in considering them as human, whereas they are only masculine.

Play, in the childish sense is an expression of previous habit; and to be studied in that light. Play in the educational sense should be encouraged or discouraged to develop desired characteristics. This we know, and practice; only we do it under androcentric canons; confining the girl to the narrow range we consider proper for women, and assisting the boy to cover life with the expression of masculinity, when we should be helping both to a more human development.

Our settled conviction that men are people—the people, and that masculine qualities are the main desideratam in life, is what keeps up this false estimate of the value of our present games. Advocates of football, for instance, proudly claim that it fits a man for life. Life—from the wholly male point of view—is a battle, with a prize. To want something beyond measure, and to fight to get—that is the simple proposition. This view of life finds its most naive expression in predatory warfare; and still tends to make predatory warfare of the later and more human processes of industry. Because they see life in this way they imagine that skill and practice in the art of fighting, especially in collective fighting, is so valuable in our modern life. This is an archaism which would be laughable if it were not so dangerous in its effects.

The valuable processes to-day are those of invention, discovery, all grades of industry, and, most especially needed, the capacity for honest service and administration of our immense advantages. These are not learned on the football field. This spirit of desire and combat may be seen further in all parts of this great subject. It has developed into a cult of sportsmanship; so universally accepted among men as of superlative merit as to quite blind them to other standards of judgment.

In the Cook-Peary controversy of 1909, this canon was made manifest. Here, one man had spent a lifetime in trying to accomplish something; and at the eleventh hour succeeded. Then, coming out in the rich triumph long deferred, he finds another man, of character well known to him, impudently and falsely claiming that he had done it first. Mr. Peary expressed himself, quite restrainedly and correctly, in regard to the effrontery and falsity of this claim—and all the country rose up and denounced him as "unsportsmanlike!"

Sport and the canons of sport are so dominant in the masculine mind that what they considered a deviation from these standards was of far more importance than the question of fact involved; to say nothing of the moral obliquity of one lying to the whole world, for money; and that at the cost of another's hard-won triumph.

If women had condemned the conduct of one or the other as "not good house-wifery," this would have been considered a most puerile comment. But to be "unsportsmanlike" is the unpardonable sin.

Owing to our warped standards we glaringly misjudge the attitude of the two sexes in regard to their amusements. Of late years more women than ever before have taken to playing cards; and some, unfortunately, play for money. A steady stream of comment and blame follows upon this. The amount of card playing among men—and the amount of money lost and won, does not produce an equivalent comment.

Quite aside from this one field of dissipation, look at the share of life, of time, of strength, of money, given by men to their wide range of recreation. The primitive satisfaction of hunting and fishing they maintain at enormous expense. This is the indulgence of a most rudimentary impulse; pre-social and largely pre-human, of no service save as it affects bodily health, and of a most deterring influence on real human development. Where hunting and fishing is of real human service, done as a means of livelihood, it is looked down upon like any other industry; it is no longer "sport."

The human being kills to eat, or to sell and eat from the returns; he kills for the creature's hide or tusks, for use of some sort; or to protect his crops from vermin, his flocks from depredation; but the sportsman kills for the gratification of a primeval instinct, and under rules of an arbitrary cult. "Game" creatures are his prey; bird, beast or fish that is hard to catch, that requires some skill to slay; that will give him not mere meat and bones, but "the pleasure of the chase."

The pleasure of the chase is a very real one. It is exemplified, in its broad sense in children's play. The running and catching games, the hiding and finding games, are always attractive to our infancy, as they are to that of cubs and kittens. But the long continuance of this indulgence among mature civilized beings is due to their masculinity. That group of associated sex instincts, which in the woman prompts to the patient service and fierce defence of the little child, in the man has its deepest root in seeking, pursuing and catching. To hunt is more than a means of obtaining food, in his long ancestry; it is to follow at any cost, to seek through all difficulties, to struggle for and secure the central prize of his being—a mate.

His "protective instincts" are far later and more superficial. To support and care for his wife, his children, is a recent habit, in plain sight historically; but "the pleasure of the chase" is older than that. We should remember that associate habits and impulses last for ages upon ages in living forms; as in the tree climbing instincts of our earliest years, of Simian origin; and the love of water, which dates back through unmeasured time. Where for millions of years the strongest pleasure a given organism is fitted for, is obtained by a certain group of activities, those activities will continue to give pleasure long after their earlier use is gone.

This is why men enjoy "the ardor of pursuit" far more than women. It is an essentially masculine ardor. To come easily by what he wants does not satisfy him. He wants to want it. He wants to hunt it, seek it, chase it, catch it. He wants it to be "game." He is by virtue of his sex a sportsman.

There is no reason why these special instincts should not be gratified so long as it does no harm to the more important social processes; but it is distinctly desirable that we should understand their nature. The reason why we have the present overwhelming mass of "sporting events," from the ball game to the prize fight, is because our civilization is so overwhelmingly masculine. We shall criticize them more justly when we see that all this mass of indulgence is in the first place a form of sex-expression, and in the second place a survival of instincts older than the oldest savagery.

Besides our games and sports we have a large field of "amusements" also worth examining. We not only enjoy doing things, but we enjoy seeing them done by others. In these highly specialized days most of our amusement consists in paying two dollars to sit three hours and see other people do things.

This in its largest sense is wholly human. We, as social creatures, can enjoy a thousand forms of expression quite beyond the personal. The birds must each sing his own song; the crickets chirp in millionfold performance; but human being feels the deep thrill of joy in their special singers, actors, dancers, as well as in their own personal attempts. That we should find pleasure in watching one another is humanly natural, but what it is we watch, the kind of pleasure and the kind of performance, opens a wide field of choice.

We know, for instance, something of the crude excesses of aboriginal Australian dances; we know more of the gross license of old Rome; we know the breadth of the jokes in medieval times, and the childish brutality of the bull-ring and the cockpit. We know, in a word, that amusements vary; that they form a ready gauge of character and culture; that they have a strong educational influence for good or bad. What we have not hitherto observed is the predominant masculine influence on our amusements. If we recall once more the statement with regard to entertaining anecdotes, "There are thirty good stories in the world, and twenty-nine of them cannot be told to women," we get a glaring sidelight on the masculine specialization in jokes.

"Women have no sense of humor" has been frequently said, when "Women have not a masculine sense of humor" would be truer. If women had thirty "good stories" twenty-nine of which could not be told to men, it is possible that men, if they heard some of the twenty-nine, would not find them funny. The overweight of one sex has told in our amusements as everywhere else.

Because men are further developed in humanity than women are as yet, they have built and organized great places of amusement; because they carried into their humanity their unchecked masculinity, they have made these amusements to correspond. Dramatic expression, is in its true sense, not only a human distinction, but one of our noblest arts. It is allied with the highest emotions; is religious, educational, patriotic, covering the whole range of human feeling. Through it we should be able continually to express, in audible, visible forms, alive and moving, whatever phase of life we most enjoyed or wished to see. There was a time when the drama led life; lifted, taught, inspired, enlightened. Now its main function is to amuse. Under the demand for amusement, it has cheapened and coarsened, and now the thousand vaudevilles and picture shows give us the broken fragments of a degraded art of which our one main demand is that it shall make us laugh.

There are many causes at work here; and while this study seeks to show in various fields one cause, it does not claim that cause is the only one. Our economic conditions have enormous weight upon our amusements, as on all other human phenomena; but even under economic pressure the reactions of men and women are often dissimilar. Tired men and women both need amusement, the relaxation and restful change of irresponsible gayety. The great majority of women, who work longer hours than any other class, need it desperately and never get it. Amusement, entertainment, recreation, should be open to us all, enjoyed by all. This is a human need, and not a distinction of either sex. Like most human things it is not only largely monopolized by men, but masculized throughout. Many forms of amusement are for men only; more for men mostly; all are for men if they choose to go.

The entrance of women upon the stage, and their increased attendance at theatres has somewhat modified the nature of the performance; even the "refined vaudeville" now begins to show the influence of women. It would be no great advantage to have this department of human life feminized; the improvement desired is to have it less masculized; to reduce the excessive influence of one, and to bring out those broad human interests and pleasures which men and women can equally participate in and enjoy.

VII

ETHICS AND RELIGION

The laws of physics were at work before we were on earth, and continued to work on us long before we had intelligence enough to perceive, much less understand, them. Our proven knowledge of these processes constitutes "the science of physics"; but the laws were there before the science.

Physics is the science of material relation, how things and natural forces work with and on one another. Ethics is the science of social relation, how persons and social forces work with and on one another.

Ethics is to the human world what physics is to the material world; ignorance of ethics leaves us in the same helpless position in regard to one another that ignorance of physics left us in regard to earth, air, fire and water.

To be sure, people lived and died and gradually improved, while yet ignorant of the physical sciences; they developed a rough "rule of thumb" method, as animals do, and used great forces without understanding them. But their lives were safer and their improvement more rapid as they learned more, and began to make servants of the forces which had been their masters.

We have progressed, lamely enough, with terrible loss and suffering, from stark savagery to our present degree of civilization; we shall go on more safely and swiftly when we learn more of the science of ethics.

Let us note first that while the underlying laws of ethics remain steady and reliable, human notions of them have varied widely and still do so. In different races, ages, classes, sexes, different views of ethics obtain; the conduct of the people is modified by their views, and their prosperity is modified by their conduct.

Primitive man became very soon aware that conduct was of importance. As consciousness increased, with the power to modify action from within, instead of helplessly reacting to stimuli from without, there arose the crude first codes of ethics, the "Thou shalt" and "Thou shalt not" of the blundering savage. It was mostly "Thou shalt not." Inhibition, the checking of an impulse proven disadvantageous, was an earlier and easier form of action than the later human power to consciously decide on and follow a course of action with no stimulus but one's own will.

Primitive ethics consists mostly of Tabus—the things that are forbidden; and all our dim notions of ethics to this day, as well as most of our religions, deal mainly with forbidding.

This is almost the whole of our nursery government, to an extent shown by the well-worn tale of the child who said her name was "Mary." "Mary what?" they asked her. And she answered, "Mary Don't." It is also the main body of our legal systems—a complex mass of prohibitions and preventions. And even in manners and conventions, the things one should not do far outnumber the things one should. A general policy of negation colors our conceptions of ethics and religion.

When the positive side began to be developed, it was at first in purely arbitrary and artificial form. The followers of a given religion were required to go through certain motions, as prostrating themselves, kneeling, and the like; they were required to bring tribute to the gods and their priests, sacrifices, tithes, oblations; they were set little special performances to go through at given times; the range of things forbidden was broad; the range of things commanded was narrow. The Christian religion, practically interpreted, requires a fuller "change of heart" and change of life than any preceding it; which may account at once for its wide appeal to enlightened peoples, and to its scarcity of application.

Again, in surveying the field, it is seen that as our grasp of ethical values widened, as we called more and more acts and tendencies "right" and "wrong," we have shown astonishing fluctuations and vagaries in our judgment. Not only in our religions, which have necessarily upheld each its own set of prescribed actions as most "right," and its own special prohibitions as most "wrong"; but in our beliefs about ethics and our real conduct, we have varied absurdly.

Take, for instance, the ethical concept among "gentlemen" a century or so since, which put the paying of one's gambling debts as a well-nigh sacred duty, and the paying of a tradesman who had fed and clothed one as a quite negligible matter. If the process of gambling was of social service, and the furnishing of food and clothes was not, this might be good ethics; but as the contrary is true, we have to account for this peculiar view on other grounds.

Again, where in Japan a girl, to maintain her parents, is justified in leading a life of shame, we have a peculiar ethical standard difficult for

Western minds to appreciate. Yet in such an instance as is described in "Auld Robin Gray," we see precisely the same code; the girl, to benefit her parents, marries a rich old man she does not love—which is to lead a life of shame. The ethical view which justifies this, puts the benefit of parents above the benefit of children, robs the daughter of happiness and motherhood, injures posterity to assist ancestors.

This is one of the products of that very early religion, ancestor worship; and here we lay a finger on a distinctly masculine influence.

We know little of ethical values during the matriarchate; whatever they were, they must have depended for sanction on a cult of promiscuous but efficient maternity. Our recorded history begins in the patriarchal period, and it is its ethics alone which we know.

The mother instinct, throughout nature, is one of unmixed devotion, of love and service, care and defence, with no self-interest. The animal father, in such cases as he is of service to the young, assists the mother in her work in similar fashion. But the human father in the family with the male head soon made that family an instrument of desire, and combat, and self-expression, following the essentially masculine impulses. The children were his, and if males, valuable to serve and glorify him. In his dominance over servile women and helpless children, free rein was given to the growth of pride and the exercise of irresponsible tyranny. To these feelings, developed without check for thousands of years, and to the mental habits resultant, it is easy to trace much of the bias of our early ethical concepts.

Perhaps it is worth while to repeat here that the effort of this book is by no means to attribute a wholly evil influence to men, and a wholly good one to women; it is not even claimed that a purely feminine culture would have advanced the world more successfully. It does claim that the influence of the two together is better than that of either one alone; and in especial to point out what special kind of injury is due to the exclusive influence of one sex heretofore.

We have to-day reached a degree of human development where both men and women are capable of seeing over and across the distinctions of sex, and mutually working for the advancement of the world. Our progress is, however, seriously impeded by what we may call the masculine tradition, the unconscious dominance of a race habit based on this long androcentric period; and it is well worth while, in the interests of both sexes, to show the mischievous effects of the predominance of one.

We have in our ethics not only a "double standard" in one special line, but in nearly all. Man, as a sex, has quite naturally deified his own qualities rather than those of his opposite. In his codes of manners, of morals, of laws, in his early concepts of God, his ancient religions, we see masculinity written large on every side. Confining women wholly to their feminine functions, he has required of them only what he called feminine virtues, and the one virtue he has demanded, to the complete overshadowing of all others, is measured by wholly masculine requirements.

In the interests of health and happiness, monogamous marriage proves its superiority in our racc as it has in others. It is essential to the best growth of humanity that we practice the virtue of chastity; it is a human virtue, not a feminine one. But in masculine hands this virtue was enforced upon women under penalties of hideous cruelty, and quite ignored by men. Masculine ethics, colored by masculine instincts, always dominated by sex, has at once recognized the value of chastity in the woman, which is right; punished its absence unfairly, which is wrong; and then reversed the whole matter when applied to men, which is ridiculous.

Ethical laws are laws—not idle notions. Chastity is a virtue because it promotes human welfare—not because men happen to prize it in women and ignore it themselves. The underlying reason for the whole thing is the benefit of the child; and to that end a pure and noble fatherhood is requisite, as well as such a motherhood. Under the limitations of a too masculine ethics, we have developed on this one line social conditions which would be absurdly funny if they were not so horrible.

Religion, be it noticed, does not bear out this attitude. The immense human need of religion, the noble human character of the great religious teachers, has always set its standards, when first established, ahead of human conduct.

Some there are, men of learning and authority, who hold that the deadening immobility of our religions, their resistance to progress and relentless preservation of primitive ideals, is due to the conservatism of women. Men, they say, are progressive by nature; women are conservative. Women are more religious than men, and so preserve old religious forms unchanged after men have outgrown them.

If we saw women in absolute freedom, with a separate religion devised by women, practiced by women, and remaining unchanged through the centuries; while men, on the other hand, bounded bravely forward, making new ones as fast as they were needed, this belief might be maintained. But what do we see? All the old religions made by men, and forced on the women whether they liked it or not. Often women not even considered as part of the scheme—denied souls—given a much lower place in the system—going from the service of their father's gods to the service of their husbands—having none of their own. We see religions which make practically no place for women, as with the Moslem, as rigidly bigoted and unchanging as any other.

We see also this: that the wider and deeper the religion, the more human, the more it calls for practical applications in Christianity—the more it appeals to women. Further, in the diverging sects of the Christian religion, we find that its progressiveness is to be measured, not by the numbers of its women adherents, but by their relative freedom. The women of America, who belong to a thousand sects, who follow new ones with avidity, who even make them, and who also leave them all as men do, are women, as well as those of Spain, who remain contented Romanists, but in America the status of women is higher.

The fact is this: a servile womanhood is in a state of arrested development, and as such does form a ground for the retention of ancient ideas. But this is due to the condition of servility, not to womanhood. That women at present are the bulwark of the older forms of our religions is due to the action of two classes of men: the men of the world, who keep women in their restricted position, and the men of the church, who take every advantage of the limitations of women. When we have for the first time in history a really civilized womanhood, we can then judge better of its effect on religion.

Meanwhile, we can see quite clearly the effect of manhood. Keeping in mind those basic masculine impulses—desire and combat—we see them reflected from high heaven in their religious concepts. Reward! Something to want tremendously and struggle to achieve! This is a concept perfectly masculine and most imperfectly religious. A religion is partly explanation—a theory of life; it is partly emotion—an attitude of mind, it is partly action—a system of morals. Man's special effect on this large field of human development is clear. He pictured his early gods as like to himself, and they behaved in accordance with his ideals. In the dimmest, oldest religions, nearest the matriarchate, we find great goddesses—types of Motherhood, Mother-love, Mother-care and Service. But under masculine dominance, Isis and Ashteroth dwindle away to an alluring Aphrodite—not Womanhood for the child and the World—but the incarnation of female attractiveness for man.

As the idea of heaven developed in the man's mind it became the Happy Hunting Ground of the savage, the beery and gory Valhalla of the Norseman, the voluptuous, many-houri-ed Paradise of the Mohammedan. These are men's heavens all. Women have never been so fond of hunting, beer or blood; and their houris would be of the other kind. It may be said that the early Christian idea of heaven is by no means planned for men. That is trite, and is perhaps the reason why it has never had so compelling an attraction for them.

Very early in his vague efforts towards religious expression, man voiced his second strongest instinct—that of combat. His universe is always dual, always a scene of combat. Born with that impulse, exercising it continually, he naturally assumed it to be the major process in life. It is not. Growth is the major process. Combat is a useful subsidiary process, chiefly valuable for its initial use, to transmit the physical superiority of the victor. Psychic and social advantages are not thus secured or transmitted.

In no one particular is the androcentric character of our common thought more clearly shown than in the general deification of what are now described as "conflict stimuli." That which is true of the male creature as such is assumed to be true of life in general; quite naturally, but by no means correctly. To this universal masculine error we may trace in the field of religion and ethics the great devil theory, which has for so long obscured our minds. A God without an Adversary was inconceivable to the masculine mind. From this basic misconception we find all our ideas of ethics distorted; that which should have been treated as a group of truths to be learned and habits to be cultivated was treated in terms of combat, and moral growth made an everlasting battle. This combat theory we may follow later into our common notions of discipline, government, law and punishment; here is it enough to see its painful effects in this primary field of ethics and religion?

The third essential male trait of self-expression we may follow from its innocent natural form in strutting cock or stamping stag up to the characteristics we label vanity and pride. The degradation of women in forcing them to adopt masculine methods of personal decoration as a means of livelihood, has carried with the concomitant of personal vanity: but to this day and at their worst we do not find in women the *naive* exultant glow of pride which swells the bosom of the men who march in procession with brass bands, in full regalia of any sort, so that it be gorgeous, exhibiting their glories to all.

It is this purely masculine spirit which has given to our early concepts of Deity the unadmirable qualities of boundless pride and a thirst for constant praise and prostrate admiration, characteristics certainly unbefitting any noble idea of God. Desire, combat and self-expression all have had their unavoidable influence on masculine religions. What deified Maternity a purely feminine culture might have put forth we do not know, having had none such. Women are generally credited with as much moral sense as men, and as much religious instinct; but so far it has had small power to modify our prevailing creeds.

As a matter of fact, no special sex attributes should have any weight in our ideas of right and wrong. Ethics and religion are distinctly human concerns; they belong to us as social factors, not as physical ones. As we learn to recognize our humanness, and to leave our sex characteristics where they belong, we shall at last learn something about ethics as a simple and practical science, and see that religions grow as the mind grows to formulate them.

If anyone seeks for a clear, simple, easily grasped proof of our ethics, it is to be found in a popular proverb. Struggling upward from beast and savage into humanness, man has seen, reverenced, and striven to attain various human virtues.

He was willing to check many primitive impulses, to change many barbarous habits, to manifest newer, nobler powers. Much he would concede to Humanness, but not his sex—that was beyond the range of Ethics or Religion. By the state of what he calls "morals," and the laws he makes to regulate them, by his attitude in courtship and in marriage, and by the gross anomaly of militarism, in all its senseless waste of life and wealth and joy, we may perceive this little masculine exception:

"All's fair in love and war."

VIII

EDUCATION

The origin of education is maternal. The mother animal is seen to teach her young what she knows of life, its gains and losses; and, whether consciously done or not, this is education. In our human life, education, even in its present state, is the most important process. Without it we could not maintain ourselves, much less dominate and improve conditions as we do; and when education is what it should be, our power will increase far beyond present hopes.

In lower animals, speaking generally, the powers of the race must be lodged in each individual. No gain of personal experience is of avail to the others. No advantages remain, save those physically transmitted. The narrow limits of personal gain and personal inheritance rigidly hem in sub-human progress. With us, what one learns may be taught to the others. Our life is social, collective. Our gain is for all, and profits us in proportion as we extend it to all. As the human soul develops in us, we become able to grasp more fully our common needs and advantages; and with this growth has come the extension of education to the people as a whole. Social functions are developed under natural laws, like physical ones, and may be studied similarly.

In the evolution of this basic social function, what has been the effect of wholly masculine influence?

The original process, instruction of individual child by individual mother, has been largely neglected in our man-made world. That was considered as a subsidiary sex-function of the woman, and as such, left to her "instinct." This is the main reason why we show such great progress in education for older children, and especially for youths, and so little comparatively in that given to little ones.

We have had on the one side the natural current of maternal education, with its first assistant, the nursemaid, and its second, the "dame-school"; and on the other the influence of the dominant class, organized in university, college, and public school, slowly filtering downward.

Educational forces are many. The child is born into certain conditions, physical and psychic, and "educated" thereby. He grows up into social, political and economic conditions, and is further modified by them. All these conditions, so far, have been of androcentric character; but what we call education as a special social process is what the child is deliberately taught and subjected to; and it is here we may see the same dominant influence so clearly.

This conscious education was, for long, given to boys alone, the girls being left to maternal influence, each to learn what her mother knew, and no more. This very clear instance of the masculine theory is glaring enough by itself to rest a case on. It shows how absolute was the assumption that the world was composed of men, and men alone were to be fitted for it. Women were no part of the world, and needed no training for its uses. As females they were born and not made; as human beings they were only servants, trained as such by their servant mothers.

This system of education we are outgrowing more swiftly with each year. The growing humanness of women, and its recognition, is forcing an equal education for boy and girl. When this demand was first made, by women of unusual calibre, and by men sufficiently human to overlook sex-prejudice, how was it met? What was the attitude of woman's "natural protector" when she began to ask some share in human life?

Under the universal assumption that men alone were humanity, that the world was masculine and for men only, the efforts of the women were met as a deliberate attempt to "unsex" themselves and become men. To be a woman was to be ignorant, uneducated; to be wise, educated, was to be a man. Women were not men, visibly; therefore they could not be educated, and ought not to want to be.

Under this androcentric prejudice, the equal extension of education to women was opposed at every step, and is still opposed by many. Seeing in women only sex, and not humanness, they would confine her exclusively to feminine interests. This is the masculine view, *par excellence*. In spite of it, the human development of women, which so splendidly characterizes our age, has gone on; and now both woman's colleges and those for both sexes offer "the higher education" to our girls, as well as the lower grades in school and kindergarten.

In the special professional training, the same opposition was experienced, even more rancorous and cruel. One would think that on the entrance of a few straggling and necessarily inferior feminine beginners into a trade or profession, those in possession would extend to them the right hand of fellowship, as comrades, extra assistance as beginners, and special courtesy as women.

The contrary occurred. Women were barred out, discriminated against, taken advantage of, as competitors; and as women they have had to meet special danger and offence instead of special courtesy. An unforgettable instance of this lies in the attitude of the medical colleges toward women students. The men, strong enough, one would think, in numbers, in knowledge, in established precedent, to be generous, opposed the newcomers first with absolute refusal; then, when the patient, persistent applicants did get inside, both students and teachers met them not only with unkindness and unfairness, but with a weapon ingeniously well chosen, and most discreditable—namely, obscenity. Grave professors, in lecture and clinic, as well as grinning students, used offensive language, and played offensive tricks, to drive the women out—a most androcentric performance.

Remember that the essential masculine attitude is one of opposition, of combat; his desire is obtained by first overcoming a competitor; and then see how this dominant masculinity stands out where it has no possible use or benefit—in the field of education. All along the line, man, long master of a subject sex, fought every step of woman toward mental equality. Nevertheless, since modern man has become human enough to be just, he has at last let her have a share in the advantages of education; and she has proven her full power to appreciate and use these advantages.

Then to-day rises a new cry against "women in education." Here is Mr. Barrett Wendell, of Harvard, solemnly claiming that teaching women weakens the intellect of the teacher, and every now and then bursts out a frantic sputter of alarm over the "feminization" of our schools. It is true that the majority of teachers are now women. It is true that they do have an influence on growing children. It would even seem to be true that that is largely what women are for.

But the male assumes his influence to be normal, human, and the female influence as wholly a matter of sex; therefore, where women teach boys, the boys become "effeminate"—a grievous fall. When men teach girls, do the girls become—? Here again we lack the analogue. Never has it occurred to the androcentric mind to conceive of such a thing as being too masculine. There is no such word! It is odd to notice that which ever way the woman is placed, she is supposed to exert this degrading influence; if the teacher, she effeminizes her pupils; if the pupil, she effeminizes her teachers.

Now let us shake ourselves free, if only for a moment, from the androcentric habit of mind.

As a matter of sex, the female is the more important. Her share of the processes which sex distinction serves is by far the greater. To be feminine—if one were nothing else, is a far more extensive and dignified office than to be masculine—and nothing else.

But as a matter of humanity the male of our species is at present far ahead of the female. By this superior humanness, his knowledge, his skill, his experience, his organization and specialization, he makes and manages the world. All this is human, not male. All this is as open to the woman as the man by nature, but has been denied her during our androcentric culture.

But even if, in a purely human process, such as education, she does bring her special feminine characteristics to bear, what are they, and what are the results?

We can see the masculine influence everywhere still dominant and superior. There is the first spur, Desire, the base of the reward system, the incentive of self-interest, the attitude which says, "Why should I make an effort unless it will give me pleasure?" with its concomitant laziness, unwillingness to work without payment. There is the second spur, Combat, the competitive system, which sets one against another, and finds pleasure not in learning, not exercising the mind, but in getting ahead of one's fellows. Under these two wholly masculine influences we have made the educational process a joy to the few who successfully attain, and a weary effort, with failure and contumely attached, to all the others. This may be a good method in sex-competition, but is wholly out of place and mischievous in education. Its prevalence shows the injurious masculization of this noble social process.

What might we look for in a distinctly feminine influence? What are these much-dreaded feminine characteristics?

The maternal ones, of course. The sex instincts of the male are of a preliminary nature, leading merely to the union preceding parenthood. The sex instincts of the female cover a far larger field, spending themselves most fully in the lasting love, the ceaseless service, the ingenuity and courage of efficient motherhood. To feminize education would be to make it more motherly. The mother does not rear her children by a system of prizes to be longed for and pursued; nor does she set them to compete with one another, giving to the conquering child what he needs, and to the vanquished, blame and deprivation. That would be "unfeminine."

Motherhood does all it knows to give to each child what is most needed, to teach all to their fullest capacity, to affectionately and efficiently develop the whole of them.

But this is not what is meant by those who fear so much the influence of women. Accustomed to a wholly male standard of living, to masculine ideals, virtues, methods and conditions, they say—and say with some justice—that feminine methods and ideals would be destructive to what they call "manliness." For instance, education to-day is closely interwoven with games and sports, all of an excessively masculine nature. "The education of a boy is carried on largely on the playground!" say the objectors to women teachers. Women cannot join them there; therefore, they cannot educate them.

What games are these in which women cannot join? There are forms of fighting, of course, violent and fierce, modern modifications of the instinct of sex-combat. It is quite true that women are not adapted, or inclined, to baseball or football or any violent game. They are perfectly competent to take part in all normal athletic development, the human range of agility and skill is open to them, as everyone knows who has been to the circus; but they are not built for physical combat; nor do they find ceaseless pleasure in throwing, hitting or kicking things.

But is it true that these strenuous games have the educational value attributed to them? It seems like blasphemy to question it. The whole range of male teachers, male pupils, male critics and spectators, are loud in their admiration for the "manliness" developed by the craft, courage, co-ordinative power and general "sportsmanship" developed by the game of football, for instance; that a few young men are killed and many maimed, is nothing in comparison to these advantages.

Let us review the threefold distinction on which this whole study rests, between masculine, feminine and human. Grant that woman, being feminine, cannot emulate man in being masculine—and does not want to. Grant that the masculine qualities have their use and value, as well as feminine ones. There still remain the human qualities shared by both, owned by neither, most important of all. Education is a human process, and should develop human qualities—not sex qualities. Surely our boys are sufficiently masculine, without needing a special education to make them more so.

The error lies here. A strictly masculine world, proud of its own sex and despising the other, seeing nothing in the world but sex, either male or female, has "viewed with alarm" the steady and rapid growth of humanness. Here, for instance, is a boy visibly tending to be an artist, a musician, a scientific discoverer. Here is another boy not particularly clever in any line, nor ambitious for any special work, though he means in a general way to "succeed"; he is, however, a big, husky fellow, a good fighter, mischievous as a monkey, and strong in the virtues covered by the word "sportsmanship." This boy we call "a fine manly fellow."

We are quite right. He is. He is distinctly and excessively male, at the expense of his humanness. He may make a more prepotent sire than the other, though even that is not certain; he may, and probably will, appeal more strongly to the excessively feminine girl, who has even less humanness than he; but he is not therefore a better citizen.

The advance of civilization calls for human qualities, in both men and women. Our educational system is thwarted and hindered, not as Prof. Wendell and his life would have us believe, by "feminization," but by an overweening masculization.

Their position is a simple one. "We are men. Men are human beings. Women are only women. This is a man's world. To get on in it you must do it man-fashion—i.e., fight, and overcome the others. Being civilized, in part, we must arrange a sort of 'civilized warfare,' and learn to play the game, the old crude, fierce male game of combat, and we must educate our boys thereto." No wonder education was denied to women. No wonder their influence is dreaded by an ultra-masculine culture.

It will change the system in time. It will gradually establish an equal place in life for the feminine characteristics, so long belittled and derided, and give pre-eminent dignity to the human power.

Physical culture, for both boys and girls, will be part of such a modified system. All things that both can do together will be accepted as human; but what either boys or girls have to retire apart to practice will be frankly called masculine and feminine, and not encouraged in children.

The most important qualities are the human ones, and will be so named and honored. Courage is a human quality, not a sex-quality. What is commonly called courage in male animals is mere belligerence, the fighting instinct. To meet an adversary of his own sort is a universal masculine trait; two father cats may fight fiercely each other, but both will run from a dog as quickly as a mother cat. She has courage enough, however, in defence of her kittens.

What this world most needs to-day in both men and women, is the power to recognize our public conditions; to see the relative importance of measures; to learn the processes of constructive citizenship. We need an education which shall give its facts in the order of their importance; morals and manners based on these facts; and train our personal powers with careful selection, so that each may best serve the community.

At present, in the larger processes of extra-scholastic education, the advantage is still with the boy. From infancy we make the gross mistake of accentuating sex in our children, by dress and all its limitations, by special teaching of what is "ladylike" and "manly." The boy is allowed a freedom of experience far beyond the girl. He learns more of his town and city, more of machinery, more of life, passing on from father to son the truths as well as traditions of sex superiority.

All this is changing before our eyes, with the advancing humanness of women. Not yet, however, has their advance affected, to any large extent, the base of all education; the experience of a child's first years. Here is where the limitations of women have checked race progress most thoroughly. Here hereditary influence was constantly offset by the advance of the male. Social selection did develop higher types of men, though sex-selection reversed still insisted on primitive types of women. But the educative influence of these primitive women, acting most exclusively on the most susceptible years of life, has been a serious deterrent to race progress.

Here is the dominant male, largely humanized, yet still measuring life from male standards. He sees women only as a sex. (Note here the criticism of Europeans on American women. "Your women are so sexless!" they say, meaning merely that our women have human qualities as well as feminine.) And children he considers as part and parcel of the same domain, both inferior classes, "women and children."

I recall in Rimmer's beautiful red chalk studies, certain profiles of man, woman and child, and careful explanation that the proportion of the woman's face and head were far more akin to the child than to the man. What Mr. Rimmer should have shown, and could have, by profuse illustration, was that the faces of boy and girl differ but slightly, and the faces of old men and women differ as little, sometimes not at all; while the face of the woman approximates the human more closely than that of the man; while the child, representing race more than sex, is naturally more akin to her than to him. The male reserves more primitive qualities, the hairiness, the more pugnacious jaw; the female is nearer to the higher human types.

An ultra-male selection has chosen women for their femininity first, and next for qualities of submissiveness and patient service bred by long ages of servility.

This servile womanhood, or the idler and more excessively feminine type, has never appreciated the real power and place of the mother, and has never been able to grasp or to carry out any worthy system of education for little children. Any experienced teacher, man or woman, will own how rare it is to find a mother capable of a dispassionate appreciation of educative values. Books in infant education and child culture generally are read by teachers more than mothers, so our public libraries prove. The mother-instinct, quite suitable and sufficient in animals, is by no means equal to the requirements of civilized life. Animal motherhood furnishes a fresh wave of devotion for each new birth; primitive human motherhood extends that passionate tenderness over the growing family for a longer period; but neither can carry education beyond its rudiments.

So accustomed are we to our world-old method of entrusting the first years of the child to the action of untaught, unbridled mother-instinct, that suggestions as to a better education for babies are received with the frank derision of massed ignorance.

That powerful and brilliant writer, Mrs. Josephine Daskam Bacon, among others has lent her able pen to ridicule and obstruct the gradual awakening of human intelligence in mothers, the recognition that babies are no exception to the rest of us in being better off for competent care and service. It seems delightfully absurd to these reactionaries that ages of human progress should be of any benefit to babies, save, indeed, as their more human fathers, specialized and organized, are able to provide them with better homes and a better world to grow up in. The idea that mothers, more human, should specialize and organize as well, and extend to their babies these supreme advantages, is made a laughing stock.

It is easy and profitable to laugh with the majority; but in the judgment of history, those who do so, hold unenviable positions. The time is coming when the human mother will recognize the educative possibilities of early childhood, learn that the ability to rightly teach little children is rare and precious, and be proud and glad to avail themselves of it.

We shall then see a development of the most valuable human qualities in our children's minds such as would now seem wildly Utopian. We shall learn from wide and long experience to anticipate and provide for the steps of the unfolding mind, and train it, through carefully prearranged experiences, to a power of judgment, of self-control, of social perception, now utterly unthought of.

Such an education would begin at birth; yes, far before it, in the standards of a conscious human motherhood. It would require a quite different status of wifehood, womanhood, girlhood. It would be wholly impossible if we were never to outgrow our androcentric culture.

IX

"Society" and "Fashion"

Among our many naive misbeliefs is the current fallacy that "society" is made by women; and that women are responsible for that peculiar social manifestation called "fashion."

Men and women alike accept this notion; the serious essayist and philosopher, as well as the novelist and paragrapher, reflect it in their pages. The force of inertia acts in the domain of psychics as well as physics; any idea pushed into the popular mind with considerable force will keep on going until some opposing force—or the slow resistance of friction—stops it at last.

"Society" consists mostly of women. Women carry on most of its processes, therefore women are its makers and masters, they are responsible for it, that is the general belief.

We might as well hold women responsible for harems—or prisoners for jails. To be helplessly confined to a given place or condition does not prove that one has chosen it; much less made it.

No; in an androcentric culture "society," like every other social relation, is dominated by the male and arranged for his convenience. There are, of course, modifications due to the presence of the other sex; where there are more women than men there are inevitable results of their influence; but the character and conditions of the whole performance are dictated by men.

Social intercourse is the prime condition of human life. To meet, to mingle, to know one another, to exchange, not only definite ideas, facts, and feelings, but to experience that vague general stimulus and enlarged power that comes of contact—all this is essential to our happiness as well as to our progress.

This grand desideratum has always been monopolized by men as far as possible. What intercourse was allowed to women has been rigidly hemmed its by man-made conventions. Women accept these conventions, repeat them, enforce them upon their daughters; but they originate with men.

The feet of the little Chinese girl are bound by her mother and her nurse—but it is not for woman's pleasure that this crippling torture was invented. The Oriental veil is worn by women, but it is not for any need of theirs that veils were decreed them.

When we look at society in its earlier form we find that the public house has always been with us. It is as old almost as the private house; the need for association is as human as the need for privacy. But the public house was—and is—for men only. The woman was kept as far as possible at home. Her female nature was supposed to delimit her life satisfactorily, and her human stature was completely ignored.

Under the pressure of that human nature she has always rebelled at the social restrictions which surrounded her; and from the women of older lands gathered at the well, or in the market place, to our own women on the church steps or in the sewing circle, they have ceaselessly struggled for the social intercourse which was as much a law of their being as of man's.

When we come to the modern special field that we call "society," we find it to consist of a carefully arranged set of processes and places wherein women may meet one another and meet men. These vary, of course, with race, country, class, and period; from the clean licence of our western customs to the strict chaperonage of older lands; but free as it is in America, even here there are bounds.

Men associate without any limit but that of inclination and financial capacity. Even class distinction only works one way—the low-class man may not mingle with high-class women; but the high-class man may—and does—mingle with low-class women. It is his society—may not a man do what he will with his own?

Caste distinctions, as have been ably shown by Prof. Lester F. Ward, are relics of race distinction; the subordinate caste was once a subordinate race; and while mating, upward, was always forbidden to the subject race; mating, downward, was always practiced by the master race.

The elaborate shading of "the color line" in slavery days, from pure black up through mulatto, quadroon, octoroon, quinteroon, griffada, mustafee, mustee, and sang d'or—to white again; was not through white mothers—but white fathers; never too exclusive in their tastes. Even in slavery, the worst horrors were strictly androcentric.

"Society" is strictly guarded—that is its women are. As always, the main tabu is on the woman. Consider carefully the relation between "society" and the growing girl. She must, of course, marry; and her education, manners, character, must of course be pleasing to the

CHARLOTTE PERKINS GILMAN

prospective wooer. That which is desirable in young girls means, naturally, that which is desirable to men. Of all cultivated accomplishments the first is "innocence." Beauty may or may not be forthcoming; but "innocence" is "the chief charm of girlhood."

Why? What good does it do *her?* Her whole life's success is made to depend on her marrying; her health and happiness depends on her marrying the right man. The more "innocent" she is, the less she knows, the easier it is for the wrong man to get her.

As is so feelingly described in "The Sorrows of Amelia," in "The Ladies' Literary Cabinet," a magazine taken by my grandmother; "The only foible which the delicate Amelia possessed was an unsuspecting breast to lavish esteem. Unversed in the secret villanies of a base degenerate world, she ever imagined all mankind to be as spotless as herself. Alas for Amelia! This fatal credulity was the source of all her misfortunes." It was. It is yet.

Just face the facts with new eyes—look at it as if you had never seen "society" before; and observe the position of its "Queen."

Here is Woman. Let us grant that Motherhood is her chief purpose. (As a female it is. As a human being she has others!) Marriage is our way of safeguarding motherhood; of ensuring "support" and "protection" to the wife and children.

"Society" is very largely used as a means to bring together young people, to promote marriage. If "society" is made and governed by women we should naturally look to see its restrictions and encouragements such as would put a premium on successful maternity and protect women—and their children—from the evils of ill-regulated fatherhood.

Do we find this? By no means.

"Society" allows the man all liberty—all privilege—all license. There are certain offences which would exclude him; such as not paying gambling debts, or being poor; but offences against womanhood—against motherhood—do not exclude him.

How about the reverse?

If "society" is made by women, for women, surely a misstep by a helplessly "innocent" girl, will not injure her standing!

But it does. She is no longer "innocent." She knows now. She has lost her market value and is thrown out of the shop. Why not? It is his shop—not hers. What women may and may not be, what they must and must not do, all is measured from the masculine standard.

A really feminine "society" based on the needs and pleasures of women, both as females and as human beings, would in the first place accord them freedom and knowledge; the knowledge which is power. It would not show us "the queen of the ballroom" in the position of a wall-flower unless favored by masculine invitation; unable to eat unless he brings her something; unable to cross the floor without his arm. Of all blind stultified "royal sluggards" she is the archetype. No, a feminine society would grant *at least* equality to women in this, their so-called special field.

Its attitude toward men, however, would be rigidly critical.

Fancy a real Mrs. Grundy (up to date it has been a Mr., his whiskers hid in capstrings) saying, "No, no, young man. You won't do. You've been drinking. The habit's growing on you. You'll make a bad husband."

Or still more severely, "Out with you, sir! You've forfeited your right to marry! Go into retirement for seven years, and when you come back bring a doctor's certificate with you."

That sounds ridiculous, doesn't it—for "Society" to say? It is ridiculous, in a man's "society."

The required dress and decoration of "society"; the everlasting eating and drinking of "society," the preferred amusements of "society," the absolute requirements and absolute exclusions of "society," are of men, by men, for men,—to paraphrase a threadbare quotation. And then, upon all that vast edifice of masculine influence, they turn upon women as Adam did; and blame *them* for severity with their fallen sisters! "Women are so hard upon women!"

They have to be. What man would "allow" his wife, his daughters, to visit and associate with "the fallen"? His esteem would be forfeited, they would lose their "social position," the girl's chance of marrying would be gone.

Men are not so stern. They may visit the unfortunate women, to bring them help, sympathy, re-establishment—or for other reasons; and it does not forfeit their social position. Why should it? They make the regulation.

Women are to-day, far more conspicuously than men, the exponents and victims of that mysterious power we call "Fashion." As shown in mere helpless imitation of one another's idea, customs, methods, there is not much difference; in patient acquiescence with prescribed models of architecture, furniture, literature, or anything else; there is not much difference; but in personal decoration there is a most conspicuous difference. Women do to-day submit to more grotesque ugliness and absurdity than men; and there are plenty of good reasons for it.

Confining our brief study of fashion to fashion in dress, let us observe why it is that women wear these fine clothes at all; and why they change them as they do.

First, and very clearly, the human female carries the weight of sex decoration, solely because of her economic dependence on the male. She alone in nature adds to the burdens of maternity, which she was meant for, this unnatural burden of ornament, which she was not meant for. Every other female in the world is sufficiently attractive to the male without trimmings. He carries the trimmings, sparing no expense of spreading antlers or trailing plumes; no monstrosity of crest and wattles, to win her favor.

She is only temporarily interested in him. The rest of the time she is getting her own living, and caring for her own young. But our women get their bread from their husbands, and every other social need. The woman depends on the man for her position in life, as well as the necessities of existence. For herself and for her children she must win and hold him who is the source of all supplies. Therefore she is forced to add to her own natural attractions this "dance of the seven veils," of the seventeen gowns, of the seventy-seven hats of gay delirium.

There are many who think in one syllable, who say, "women don't dress to please men—they dress to please themselves—and to outshine other women." To these I would suggest a visit to some summer shore resort during the week and extending over Saturday night. The women have all the week to please themselves and outshine one another; but their array on Saturday seems to indicate the approach of some new force or attraction.

If all this does not satisfy I would then call their attention to the well-known fact that the young damsel previous to marriage spends far more time and ingenuity in decoration than she does afterward. This has long been observed and deprecated by those who write Advice to Wives, on the ground that this difference is displeasing to the husband—that she loses her influence over him; which is true. But since his own "society," knowing his weakness, has tied him to her by law; why should she keep up what is after all an unnatural exertion?

That excellent magazine "Good Housekeeping" has been running for some months a rhymed and illustrated story of "Miss Melissa Clarissa McRae," an extremely dainty and well-dressed stenographer, who captured and married a fastidious young man, her employer, by the force of her artificial attractions—and then lost his love after marriage by a sudden unaccountable slovenliness—the same old story.

If this in not enough, let me instance further the attitude toward "Fashion" of that class of women who live most openly and directly upon the favor of men. These know their business. To continually attract the vagrant fancy of the male, nature's born "variant," they must not only pile on artificial charms, but change them constantly. They do. From the leaders of this profession comes a steady stream of changing fashions; the more extreme and bizarre, the more successful—and because they are successful they are imitated.

If men did not like changes in fashion be assured these professional men-pleasers would not change them, but since Nature's Variant tires of any face in favor of a new one, the lady who would hold her sway and cannot change her face (except in color) must needs change her hat and gown.

But the Arbiter, the Ruling Cause, he who not only by choice demands, but as a business manufactures and supplies this amazing stream of fashions; again like Adam blames the woman—for accepting what he both demands and supplies.

A further proof, if more were needed, is shown in this; that in exact proportion as women grow independent, educated, wise and free, do they become less submissive to men-made fashions. Was this improvement hailed with sympathy and admiration—crowned with masculine favor?

The attitude of men toward those women who have so far presumed to "unsex themselves" is known to all. They like women to be foolish, changeable, always newly attractive; and while women must "attract" for a living—why they do, that's all.

It is a pity. It is humiliating to any far-seeing woman to have to recognize this glaring proof of the dependent, degraded position of her sex; and it ought to be humiliating to men to see the results of their mastery. These crazily decorated little creatures do not represent womanhood.

When the artist uses the woman as the type of every highest ideal; as Justice, Liberty, Charity, Truth—he does not represent her trimmed. In any part of the world where women are even in part economically independent there we find less of the absurdities of fashion. Women who work cannot be utterly absurd.

But the idle woman, the Queen of Society, who must please men within their prescribed bounds; and those of the half-world, who must please them at any cost—these are the vehicles of fashion.

X

Law and Government

It is easy to assume that men are naturally the lawmakers and law-enforcers, under the plain historic fact that they have been such since the beginning of the patriarchate.

Back of law lies custom and tradition. Back of government lies the correlative activity of any organized group. What group-insects and group-animals evolve unconsciously and fulfill by their social instincts, we evolve consciously and fulfill by arbitrary systems called laws and governments. In this, as in all other fields of our action, we must discriminate between the humanness of the function in process of development, and the influence of the male or female upon it. Quite apart from what they may like or dislike as sexes, from their differing tastes and faculties, lies the much larger field of human progress, in which they equally participate.

On this plane the evolution of law and government proceeds somewhat as follows:—The early woman-centered group organized on maternal lines of common love and service. The early combinations of men were first a grouped predacity—organized hunting; then a grouped belligerency,—organized warfare.

By special development some minds are able to perceive the need of certain lines of conduct over others, and to make this clear to their fellows; whereby, gradually, our higher social nature establishes rules and precedents to which we personally agree to submit. The process of social development is one of progressive co-ordination.

From independent individual action for individual ends, up to interdependent social action for social ends we slowly move; the "devil" in the play being the old Ego, which has to be harmonized with the new social spirit. This social process, like all others, having been in masculine hands, we may find in it the same marks of one-sided Specialization so visible in our previous studies.

The coersive attitude is essentially male. In the ceaseless age-old struggle of sex combat he developed the desire to overcome, which is always stimulated by resistance; and in this later historic period of his supremacy, he further developed the habit of dominance and mastery.

We may instance the contrast between the conduct of a man when "in love" and while courting; in which period he falls into the natural position of his sex towards the other—namely, that of a wooer; and his behavior when, with marriage, they enter the, artificial relation of the master male and servile female. His "instinct of dominance" does not assert itself during the earlier period, which was a million times longer than the latter; it only appears in the more modern and arbitrary relation.

Among other animals monogamous union is not accompanied by any such discordant and unnatural features. However recent as this habit is when considered biologically, it is as old as civilization when we consider it historically: quite old enough to be a serious force. Under its pressure we see the legal systems and forms of government slowly evolving, the general human growth always heavily perverted by the special masculine influence. First we find the mere force of custom governing us, the *mores* of the ancient people. Then comes the gradual appearance of authority, from the purely natural leadership of the best hunter or fighter up through the unnatural mastery of the patriarch, owning and governing his wives, children, slaves and cattle, and making such rules and regulations as pleased him.

Our laws as we support them now are slow, wasteful, cumbrous systems, which require a special caste to interpret and another to enforce; wherein the average citizen knows nothing of the law, and cares only to evade it when he can, obey it when he must. In the household, that stunted, crippled rudiment of the matriarchate, where alone we can find what is left of the natural influence of woman, the laws and government, so far as she is responsible for them, are fairly simple, and bear visible relation to the common good, which relation is clearly and persistently taught.

In the larger household of city and state the educational part of the law is grievously neglected. It makes no allowance for ignorance. If a man breaks a law of which he never heard he is not excused therefore; the penalty rolls on just the same. Fancy a mother making solemn rules and regulations for her family, telling the children nothing about them, and then punishing them when they disobeyed the unknown laws!

The use of force is natural to the male; while as a human being he must needs legislate somewhat in the interests of the community, as a male being he sees no necessity for other enforcement than by penalty. To violently oppose, to fight, to trample to the earth, to triumph in loud bellowings of savage joy,—these are the primitive male instincts; and the perfectly natural social instinct which leads to peaceful persuasion, to education, to an easy harmony of action, are contemptuously ranked as "feminine," or as "philanthropic,"—which is almost as bad. "Men need stronger measures" they say proudly. Yes, but four-fifths of the world are women and children!

As a matter of fact the woman, the mother, is the first co-ordinator, legislator, administrator and executive. From the guarding and guidance of her cubs and kittens up to the longer, larger management of human youth, she is the first to consider group interests and co-relate them.

As a father the male grows to share in these original feminine functions, and with us, fatherhood having become socialized while motherhood has not, he does the best he can, alone, to do the world's mother-work in his father way.

In study of any long established human custom it is very difficult to see it clearly and dispassionately. Our minds are heavily loaded with precedent, with race-custom, with the iron weight called authority. These heavy forces reach their most perfect expression in the absolutely masculine field of warfare. The absolute authority; the brainless, voiceless obedience; the relentless penalty. Here we have male coercion at its height; law and government wholly arbitrary. The result is as might be expected, a fine machine of destruction. But destruction is not a human process—merely a male process of eliminating the unfit.

The female process is to select the fit; her elimination is negative and painless.

Greater than either is the human process, to *develop fitness.*

Men are at present far more human than women. Alone upon their self-seized thrones they have carried as best they might the burdens of the state; and the history of law and government shows them as changing slowly but irresistably in the direction of social improvement.

The ancient kings were the joyous apotheosis of masculinity. Power and Pride were theirs; Limitless Display; Boundless Self-indulgence; Irresistable Authority. Slaves and courtiers bowed before them, subjects obeyed them, captive women filled their harems. But the day of the masculine monarchy is passing, and the day of the human democracy is coming in. In a Democracy Law and Government both change. Laws are no longer imposed on the people by one above them, but are evolved from the people themselves. How absurd that the people should not be educated in the laws they make; that the trailing remnants of blind submission should still becloud their minds and make them bow down patiently under the absurd pressure of outgrown tradition!

Democratic government is no longer an exercise of arbitrary authority from one above, but is an organization for public service of the people themselves—or will be when it is really attained.

In this change government ceases to be compulsion, and becomes agreement; law ceases to be authority and becomes co-ordination. When we learn the rules of whist or chess we do not obey them because we fear to be punished if we don't, but because we want to play the game. The rules of human conduct are for our own happiness and service—any child can see that. Every child will see it when laws are simplified, based on sociology, and taught in schools. A child of ten should be considered grossly uneducated who could not rewrite the main features of the laws of his country, state, and city; and those laws should be so simple in their principles that a child of ten could understand them.

TEACHER: "What is a tax?"

CHILD: "A tax is the money we agree to pay to keep up our common advantages."

TEACHER: "Why do we all pay taxes?"

CHILD: "Because the country belongs to all of us, and we must all pay our share to keep it up."

TEACHER: "In what proportion do we pay taxes?"

CHILD: "In proportion to how much money we have." (*Sotto voce*: "Of course!")

TEACHER: "What is it to evade taxes?"

CHILD: "It is treason." (*Sotto voce*: "And a dirty mean trick.")

In masculine administration of the laws we may follow the instinctive love of battle down through the custom of "trial by combat"—only recently outgrown, to our present method, where each contending party hires a champion to represent him, and these fight it out in a wordy war, with tricks and devices of complex ingenuity, enjoying this kind of struggle as they enjoy all other kinds.

It is the old masculine spirit of government as authority which is so slow in adapting itself to the democratic idea of government as service. That it should be a representative government they grasp, but representative of what? of the common will, they say; the will of the majority;—never thinking that it is the common good, the common welfare, that government should represent.

It is the inextricable masculinity in our idea of government which so revolts at the idea of women as voters. "To govern:" that means to boss, to control, to have authority; and that only, to most minds. They cannot bear to think of the woman as having control over even their own affairs; to control is masculine, they assume. Seeing only self-interest as a natural impulse, and the ruling powers of the state as a sort of umpire, an authority to preserve the rules of the game while men fight it out forever; they see in a democracy merely a wider range of self interest, and a wider, freer field to fight in.

The law dictates the rules, the government enforces them, but the main business of life, hitherto, has been esteemed as one long fierce struggle; each man seeking for himself. To deliberately legislate for the service of all the people, to use the government as the main engine of that service, is a new process, wholly human, and difficult of development under an androcentric culture.

Furthermore they put forth those naively androcentric protests,— women cannot fight, and in case their laws were resisted by men they could not enforce them,—*therefore* they should not vote!

What they do not so plainly say, but very strongly think, is that women should not share the loot which to their minds is so large a part of politics.

Here we may trace clearly the social heredity of male government.

Fix clearly in your mind the first head-ship of man—the leader of the pack as it were—the Chief Hunter. Then the second head-ship, the Chief Fighter. Then the third head-ship, the Chief of the Family. Then the long line of Chiefs and Captains, Warlords and Landlords, Rulers and Kings.

The Hunter hunted for prey, and got it. The Fighter enriched himself with the spoils of the vanquished. The Patriarch lived on the labor of women and slaves. All down the ages, from frank piracy and robbery to the measured toll of tribute, ransom and indemnity, we see the same natural instinct of the hunter and fighter. In his hands the government is a thing to sap and wreck, to live on. It is his essential impulse to want something very much; to struggle and fight for it; to take all he can get.

Set against this the giving love that comes with motherhood; the endless service that comes of motherhood; the peaceful administration in the interest of the family that comes of motherhood. We prate much of the family as the unit of the state. If it is—why not run the state on that basis? Government by women, so far as it is influenced by their sex, would be influenced by motherhood; and that would mean care, nurture, provision, education. We have to go far down the scale for any instance of organized motherhood, but we do find it in the hymenoptera; in the overflowing industry, prosperity, peace and loving service of the ant-hill and bee-hive. These are the most highly socialized types of life, next to ours, and they are feminine types.

We as human beings have a far higher form of association, with further issues than mere wealth and propagation of the species. In this human process we should never forget that men are far more advanced than women, at present. Because of their humanness has come all the noble growth of civilization, in spite of their maleness.

As human beings both male and female stand alike useful and honorable, and should in our government be alike used and honored; but as creatures of sex, the female is fitter than the male for administration of constructive social interests. The change in governmental processes which marks our times is a change in principle. Two great movements convulse the world to-day, the woman's movement and the labor movement. Each regards the other as of less moment than itself. Both are parts of the same world-process.

We are entering upon a period of social consciousness. Whereas so far almost all of us have seen life only as individuals, and have regarded the growing strength and riches of the social body as merely so much the more to fatten on; now we are beginning to take an intelligent interest in our social nature, to understand it a little, and to begin to feel the vast increase of happiness and power that comes of real Human Life.

In this change of systems a government which consisted only of prohibition and commands; of tax collecting and making war; is rapidly giving way to a system which intelligently manages our common interests, which is a growing and improving method of universal service. Here the socialist is perfectly right in his vision of the economic welfare to be assured by the socialization of industry, though that is but part of the new development; and the individualist who opposes socialism, crying loudly for the advantage of "free competition" is but voicing the spirit of the predacious male.

So with the opposers to the suffrage of women. They represent, whether men or women, the male viewpoint. They see the woman only as a female, utterly absorbed in feminine functions, belittled and ignored as her long tutelage has made her; and they see the man as he sees himself, the sole master of human affairs for as long as we have historic record.

This, fortunately, is not long. We can now see back of the period of his supremacy, and are beginning to see beyond it. We are well under way already in a higher stage of social development, conscious, well-organized, wisely managed, in which the laws shall be simple and founded on constructive principles instead of being a set of ring-regulations within which people may fight as they will; and in which the government shall be recognized in its full use; not only the sternly dominant father, and the wisely servicable mother, but the real union of all people to sanely and economically manage their affairs.

XI

CRIME AND PUNISHMENT

The human concept of Sin has had its uses no doubt; and our special invention of a thing called Punishment has also served a purpose.

Social evolution has worked in many ways wastefully, and with unnecessary pain, but it compares very favorably with natural evolution.

As we grow wiser; as our social consciousness develops, we are beginning to improve on nature in more ways than one; a part of the same great process, but of a more highly sublimated sort.

Nature shows a world of varied and changing environment. Into this comes Life—flushing and spreading in every direction. A pretty hard time Life has of it. In the first place it is dog eat dog in every direction; the joy of the hunter and the most unjoyous fear of the hunted.

But quite outside of this essential danger, the environment waits, grim and unappeasable, and continuously destroys the innocent myriads who fail to meet the one requirement of life—Adaptation. So we must not be too severe in self-condemnation when we see how foolish, cruel, crazily wasteful, is our attitude toward crime and punishment.

We become socially conscious largely through pain, and as we begin to see how much of the pain is wholly of our own causing we are overcome with shame. But the right way for society to face its past is the same as for the individual; to see where it was wrong and stop it—but to waste no time and no emotion over past misdeeds.

What is our present state as to crime? It is pretty bad. Some say it is worse than it used to be; others that it is better. At any rate it is bad enough, and a disgrace to our civilization. We have murderers by the thousand and thieves by the million, of all kinds and sizes; we have what we tenderly call "immorality," from the "errors of youth" to the sodden grossness of old age; married, single, and mixed. We have all the old kinds of wickedness and a lot of new ones, until one marvels at the purity and power of human nature, that it should carry so much disease and still grow on to higher things.

Also we have punishment still with us; private and public; applied like a rabbit's foot, with as little regard to its efficacy. Does a child offend? Punish it! Does a woman offend? Punish her! Does a man offend? Punish him! Does a group offend? Punish them!

"What for?" some one suddenly asks.

"To make them stop doing it!"

"But they have done it!"

"To make them not do it again, then."

"But they do do it again—and worse."

"To prevent other people's doing it, then."

"But it does not prevent them—the crime keeps on. What good is your punishment?"

What indeed!

What is the application of punishment to crime? Its base, its prehistoric base, is simple retaliation; and this is by no means wholly male, let us freely admit. The instinct of resistance, of opposition, of retaliation, lies deeper than life itself. Its underlying law is the law of physics—action and reaction are equal. Life's expression of this law is perfectly natural, but not always profitable. Hit your hand on a stone wall, and the stone wall hits your hand. Very good; you learn that stone walls are hard, and govern yourself accordingly.

Conscious young humanity observed and philosophized, congratulating itself on its discernment. "A man hits me—I hit the man a little harder—then he won't do it again." Unfortunately he did do it again—a little harder still. The effort to hit harder carried on the action and reaction till society, hitting hardest of all, set up a system of legal punishment, of unlimited severity. It imprisoned, it mutilated, it tortured, it killed; it destroyed whole families, and razed contumelious cities to the ground.

Therefore all crime ceased, of course? No? But crime was mitigated, surely! Perhaps. This we have proven at last; that crime does not decrease in proportion to the severest punishment. Little by little we have ceased to raze the cities, to wipe out the families, to cut off the ears, to torture; and our imprisonment is changing from slow death and insanity to a form of attempted improvement.

But punishment as a principle remains in good standing, and is still the main reliance where it does the most harm—in the rearing of children. "Spare the rod and spoil the child" remains in belief, unmodified by the millions of children spoiled by the unspared rod.

The breeders of racehorses have learned better, but not the breeders of children. Our trouble is simply the lack of intelligence. We face the babyish error and the hideous crime in exactly the same attitude.

"This person has done something offensive."

Yes?—and one waits eagerly for the first question of the rational mind—but does not hear it. One only hears "Punish him!"

What is the first question of the rational mind?

"Why?"

Human beings are not first causes. They do not evolve conduct out of nothing. The child does this, the man does that, *because* of something; because of many things. If we do not like the way people behave, and wish them to behave better, we should, if we are rational beings, study the conditions that produce the conduct.

The connection between our archaic system of punishment and our androcentric culture is two-fold. The impulse of resistance, while, as we have seen, of the deepest natural origin, is expressed more strongly in the male than in the female. The tendency to hit back and hit harder has been fostered in him by sex-combat till it has become of great intensity. The habit of authority too, as old as our history; and the cumulative weight of all the religions and systems of law and government, have furthermore built up and intensified the spirit of retaliation and vengeance.

They have even deified this concept, in ancient religions, crediting to God the evil passions of men. As the small boy recited; "Vengeance. A mean desire to get even with your enemies: 'Vengeance is mine saith the Lord'—'I will repay.'"

The Christian religion teaches better things; better than its expositors and upholders have ever understood—much less practised.

The teaching of "Love your enemies, do good unto them that hate you, and serve them that despitefully use you and persecute you," has too often resulted, when practised at all, in a sentimental negation; a pathetically useless attitude of non-resistance. You might as well base a religion on a feather pillow!

The advice given was active; direct; concrete. "*Love!*" Love is not non-resistance. "Do good!" Doing good is not non-resistance. "Serve!" Service is not non-resistance.

Again we have an overwhelming proof of the far-reaching effects of our androcentric culture. Consider it once more. Here is one by nature combative and desirous, and not by nature intended to monopolize the management of his species. He assumes to be not only the leader, but the whole thing—to be humanity itself, and to see in woman as Grant Allen so clearly put it "Not only not the race; she is not even half the race, but a subspecies, told off for purposes of reproduction merely."

Under this monstrous assumption, his sex-attributes wholly identified with his human attributes, and overshadowing them, he has imprinted on every human institution the tastes and tendencies of the male. As a male he fought, as a male human being he fought more, and deified fighting; and in a culture based on desire and combat, loud with strident self-expression, there could be but slow acceptance of the more human methods urged by Christianity. "It is a religion for slaves and women!" said the warrior of old. (Slaves and women were largely the same thing.) "It is a religion for slaves and women" says the advocate of the Superman.

Well? Who did the work of all the ancient world? Who raised the food and garnered it and cooked it and served it? Who built the houses, the temples, the aqueducts, the city wall? Who made the furniture, the tools, the weapons, the utensils, the ornaments—made them strong and beautiful and useful? Who kept the human race going, somehow, in spite of the constant hideous waste of war, and slowly built up the real industrial civilization behind that gory show?—Why just the slaves and the women.

A religion which had attractions for the real human type is not therefore to be utterly despised by the male.

In modern history we may watch with increasing ease the slow, sure progress of our growing humanness beneath the weakening shell of an all-male dominance. And in this field of what begins in the nurse as "discipline," and ends on the scaffold as "punishment," we can clearly see that blessed change.

What is the natural, the human attribute? What does this "Love," and "Do good," and "Serve" mean? In the blundering old church, still androcentric, there was a great to-do to carry out this doctrine, in elaborate symbolism. A set of beggars and cripples, gathered for the occasion, was exhibited, and kings and cardinals went solemnly through the motions of serving them. As the English schoolboy phrased it, "Thomas Becket washed the feet of leopards."

Service and love and doing good must always remain side issues in a male world. Service and love and doing good are the spirit of motherhood, and the essence of human life.

Human life is service, and is not combat. There you have the nature of the change now upon us.

What has the male mind made of Christianity?

Desire—to save one's own soul. Combat—with the Devil. Self-expression—the whole gorgeous outpouring of pageant and display, from the jewels of the high priest's breastplate to the choir of mutilated men to praise a male Deity no woman may so serve.

What kind of mind can imagine a kind of god who would like a eunuch better than a woman?

For woman they made at last a place—the usual place—of renunciation, sacrifice and service, the Sisters of Mercy and their kind; and in that loving service the woman soul has been content, not yearning for cardinal's cape or bishop's mitre.

All this is changing—changing fast. Everywhere the churches are broadening out into more service, and the service broadening out beyond a little group of widows and fatherless, of sick and in prison, to embrace its true field—all human life. In this new attitude, how shall we face the problems of crime?

Thus: "It is painfully apparent that a certain percentage of our people do not function properly. They perform antisocial acts. Why? What is the matter with them?"

Then the heart and mind of society is applied to the question, and certain results are soon reached; others slowly worked toward.

First result. Some persons are so morally diseased that they must have hospital treatment. The world's last prison will be simply a hospital for moral incurables. They must by no means reproduce their kind,—that can be attended to at once. Some are morally diseased, but may be cured, and the best powers of society will be used to cure them. Some are only morally diseased because of the conditions in which they are born and reared, and here society can save millions at once.

An intelligent society will no more neglect its children than an intelligent mother will neglect her children; and will see as clearly that ill-fed, ill-dressed, ill-taught and vilely associated little ones must grow up gravely injured.

As a matter of fact we make our crop of criminals, just as we make our idiots, blind, crippled, and generally defective. Everyone is a baby first, and a baby is not a criminal, unless we make it so. It never would be,—in right conditions. Sometimes a pervert is born, as sometimes a two-headed calf is born, but they are not common.

The older, simpler forms of crime we may prevent with case and despatch, but how of the new ones?—big, terrible, far-reaching, wide-spread crimes, for which we have as yet no names; and before which our old system of anti-personal punishment falls helpless? What of the crimes of poisoning a community with bad food; of defiling the water; of blackening the air; of stealing whole forests? What of the crimes of working little children; of building and renting tenements that produce crime and physical disease as well? What of the crime of living on the wages of fallen women—of hiring men to ruin innocent young girls; of holding them enslaved and selling them for profit? (These things are only "misdemeanors" in a man-made world!)

And what about a crime like this; to use the public press to lie to the public for private ends? No name yet for this crime; much less a penalty.

And this: To bring worse than leprosy to an innocent clean wife who loves and trusts you?

Or this: To knowingly plant poison in an unborn child?

No names, for these; no "penalties"; no conceivable penalty that could touch them.

The whole punishment system falls to the ground before the huge mass of evil that confronts us. If we saw a procession of air ships flying over a city and dropping bombs, should we rush madly off after each one crying, "Catch him! Punish him!" or should we try to stop the procession?

The time is coming when the very word "crime" will be disused, except in poems and orations; and "punishment," the word and deed, be obliterated. We are beginning to learn a little of the nature of humanity its goodness, its beauty, its lovingness; and to see that even its stupidity is only due to our foolish old methods of education.

It is not new power, new light, new hope that we need, but *to understand what ails us.*

We know enough now, we care enough now, we are strong enough now, to make the whole world a thousand fold better in a generation; but we are shackled, chained, blinded, by old false notions. The ideas of the past, the sentiments of the past, the attitude and prejudices of the past, are in our way; and among them none more universally mischievous than this great body of ideas and sentiments, prejudices and habits, which make up the offensive network of the androcentric culture.

XII

Politics and Warfare

I go to my old dictionary, and find; "Politics, 1. The science of government; that part of ethics which has to do with the regulation and government of a nation or state, the preservation of its safety, peace and prosperity; the defence of its existence and rights against foreign control or conquest; the augmentation of its strength and resources, and the protection of its citizens in their rights; with the preservation and improvement of their morals. 2. The management of political parties; the advancement of candidates to office; in a bad sense, artful or dishonest management to secure the success of political measures or party schemes, political trickery."

From present day experience we might add, 3. Politics, practical; The art of organizing and handling men in large numbers, manipulating votes, and, in especial, appropriating public wealth.

We can easily see that the "science of government" may be divided into "pure" and "applied" like other sciences, but that it is "a part of ethics" will be news to many minds.

Yet why not? Ethics is the science of conduct, and politics is merely one field of conduct; a very common one. Its connection with Warfare in this chapter is perfectly legitimate in view of the history of politics on the one hand, and the imperative modern issues which are to-day opposed to this established combination.

There are many to-day who hold that politics need not be at all connected with warfare, and others who hold that politics is warfare from start to finish.

In order to dissociate the two ideas completely let us give a paraphrase of the above definition, applying it to domestic management;—that part of ethics which has to do with the regulation and government of a family; the preservation of its safety, peace and prosperity; the defense of its existence and rights against any strangers' interference or control; the augmentation of its strength and resources, and the protection of its members in their rights; with the preservation and improvement of their morals.

All this is simple enough, and in no way masculine; neither is it feminine, save in this; that the tendency to care for, defend and manage a group, is in its origin maternal.

In every human sense, however, politics has left its maternal base far in the background; and as a field of study and of action is as well adapted to men as to women. There is no reason whatever why men should not develop great ability in this department of ethics, and gradually learn how to preserve the safety, peace and prosperity of their nation; together with those other services as to resources, protection of citizens, and improvement of morals.

Men, as human beings, are capable of the noblest devotion and efficiency in these matters, and have often shown them; but their devotion and efficiency have been marred in this, as in so many other fields, by the constant obtrusion of an ultra-masculine tendency.

In warfare, *per se*, we find maleness in its absurdest extremes. Here is to be studied the whole gamut of basic masculinity, from the initial instinct of combat, through every form of glorious ostentation, with the loudest possible accompaniment of noise.

Primitive warfare had for its climax the possession of the primitive prize, the female. Without dogmatising on so remote a period, it may be suggested as a fair hypothesis that this was the very origin of our organized raids. We certainly find war before there was property in land, or any other property to tempt aggressors. Women, however, there were always, and when a specially androcentric tribe had reduced its supply of women by cruel treatment, or they were not born in sufficient numbers, owing to hard conditions, men must needs go farther afield after other women. Then, since the men of the other tribes naturally objected to losing their main labor supply and comfort, there was war.

Thus based on the sex impulse, it gave full range to the combative instinct, and further to that thirst for vocal exultation so exquisitely male. The proud bellowings of the conquering stag, as he trampled on his prostrate rival, found higher expression in the "triumphs" of old days, when the conquering warrior returned to his home, with victims chained to his chariot wheels, and braying trumpets.

When property became an appreciable factor in life, warfare took on a new significance. What was at first mere destruction, in the effort to defend or obtain some hunting ground or pasture; and, always, to secure the female; now coalesced with the acquisitive instinct, and the long black ages of predatory warfare closed in upon the world.

Where the earliest form exterminated, the later enslaved, and took tribute; and for century upon century the "gentleman adventurer," i.e., the primitive male, greatly preferred to acquire wealth by the simple old process of taking it, to any form of productive industry.

We have been much misled as to warfare by our androcentric literature. With a history which recorded nothing else; a literature which praised and an art which exalted it; a religion which called its central power "the God of Battles"—never the God of Workshops, mind you!—with a whole complex social structure man-prejudiced from center to circumference, and giving highest praise and honor to the Soldier; it is still hard for its to see what warfare really is in human life.

Someday wc shall have new histories written, histories of world progress, showing the slow uprising, the development, the interservice of the nations; showing the faint beautiful dawn of the larger spirit of world-consciousness, and all its benefitting growth.

We shall see people softening, learning, rising; see life lengthen with the possession of herds, and widen in rich prosperity with agriculture. Then industry, blossoming, fruiting, spreading wide; art, giving light and joy; the intellect developing with companionship and human intercourse; the whole spreading tree of social progress, the trunk of which is specialized industry, and the branches of which comprise every least and greatest line of human activity and enjoyment. This growing tree, springing up wherever conditions of peace and prosperity gave it a chance, we shall see continually hewed down to the very root by war.

To the later historian will appear throughout the ages, like some Hideous Fate, some Curse, some predetermined check, to drag down all our hope and joy and set life forever at its first steps over again, this Red Plague of War.

The instinct of combat, between males, worked advantageously so long as it did not injure the female or the young. It is a perfectly natural instinct, and therefore perfectly right, in its place; but its place is in a pre-patriarchal era. So long as the animal mother was free and competent to care for herself and her young; then it was an advantage to have "the best man win;" that is the best stag or lion; and to have the vanquished die, or live in sulky celibacy, was no disadvantage to any one but himself.

Humanity is on a stage above this plan. The best man in the social structure is not always the huskiest. When a fresh horde of ultra-male savages swarmed down upon a prosperous young civilization, killed off the more civilized males and appropriated the more civilized females; they did, no doubt, bring in a fresh physical impetus to the race; but they destroyed the civilization.

The reproduction of perfectly good savages is not the main business of humanity. Its business is to grow, socially; to develop, to improve; and warfare, at its best, retards human progress; at its worst, obliterates it.

Combat is not a social process at all; it is a physical process, a subsidiary sex process, purely masculine, intended to improve the species by the elimination of the unfit. Amusingly enough, or absurdly enough; when applied to society, it eliminates the fit, and leaves the unfit to perpetuate the race!

We require, to do our organized fighting, a picked lot of vigorous young males, the fittest we can find. The too old or too young; the sick, crippled, defective; are all left behind, to marry and be fathers; while the pick of the country, physically, is sent off to oppose the pick of another country, and kill—kill—kill!

Observe the result on the population! In the first place the balance is broken—there are not enough men to go around, at home; many women are left unmated. In primitive warfare, where women were promptly enslaved, or, at the best, polygamously married, this did not greatly matter to the population; but as civilization advances and monogamy obtains, whatever eugenic benefits may once have sprung from warfare are completely lost, and all its injuries remain.

In what we innocently call "civilized warfare" (we might as well speak of "civilized cannibalism!"), this steady elimination of the fit leaves an everlowering standard of parentage at home. It makes a widening margin of what we call "surplus women," meaning more than enough to be monogamously married; and these women, not being economically independent, drag steadily upon the remaining men, postponing marriage, and increasing its burdens.

The birth rate is lowered in quantity by the lack of husbands, and lowered in quality both by the destruction of superior stock, and by the wide dissemination of those diseases which invariably accompany the wife-lessness of the segregated males who are told off to perform our military functions.

The external horrors and wastes of warfare we are all familiar with; A. It arrests industry and all progress. B. It destroys the fruits of industry and progress. C. It weakens, hurts and kills the combatants. D. It lowers the standard of the non-combatants. Even the conquering nation is heavily injured; the conquered sometimes exterminated, or at least absorbed by the victor.

This masculine selective process, when applied to nations, does not produce the same result as when applied to single opposing animals. When little Greece was overcome it did not prove that the victors were superior, nor promote human interests in any way; it injured them.

The "stern arbitrament of war" may prove which of two peoples is the better fighter, but ft does not prove it therefor the fittest to survive.

Beyond all these more or less obvious evils, comes a further result, not enough recognized; the psychic effects of military standard of thought and feeling.

Remember that an androcentric culture has always exempted its own essential activities from the restraints of ethics,—"All's fair in love and war!" Deceit, trickery, lying, every kind of skulking underhand effort to get information; ceaseless endeavor to outwit and overcome "the enemy"; besides as cruelty and destruction; are characteristic of the military process; as well as the much praised virtues of courage, endurance and loyalty, personal and public.

Also classed as a virtue, and unquestionably such from the military point of view, is that prime factor in making and keeping an army, obedience.

See how the effect of this artificial maintenance of early mental attitudes acts on our later development. True human progress requires elements quite other than these. If successful warfare made one nation unquestioned master of the earth its social progress would not be promoted by that event. The rude hordes of Genghis Khan swarmed over Asia and into Europe, but remained rude hordes; conquest is not civilization, nor any part of it.

When the northern tribes-men overwhelmed the Roman culture they paralysed progress for a thousand years or so; set back the clock by that much. So long as all Europe was at war, so long the arts and sciences sat still, or struggled in hid corners to keep their light alive.

When warfare itself ceases, the physical, social and psychic results do not cease. Our whole culture is still hag-ridden by military ideals.

Peace congresses have begun to meet, peace societies write and talk, but the monuments to soldiers and sailors (naval sailors of course), still go up, and the tin soldier remains a popular toy. We do not see boxes of tin carpenters by any chance; tin farmers, weavers, shoemakers; we do not write our "boys books" about the real benefactors and servers of society; the adventurer and destroyer remains the idol of an Androcentric Culture.

In politics the military ideal, the military processes, are so predominant as to almost monopolise "that part of ethics." The science of government, the plain wholesome business of managing a community for its own good; doing its work, advancing its prosperity, improving its morals—this is frankly understood and accepted as A Fight from start to finish. Marshall your forces and try to get in, this is the political campaign. When you are in, fight to stay in, and to keep the other fellow out. Fight for your own hand, like an animal; fight for your master like any hired bravo; fight always for some desired "victory"—and "to the victors belong the spoils."

This is not by any means the true nature of politics. It is not even a fair picture of politics to-day; in which man, the human being, is doing noble work for humanity; but it is the effect of man, the male, on politics.

Life, to the "male mind" (we have heard enough of the "female mind" to use the analogue!) *is* a fight, and his ancient military institutions and processes keep up the delusion.

As a matter of fact life is growth. Growth comes naturally, by multiplication of cells, and requires three factors to promote it; nourishment, use, rest. Combat is a minor incident of life; belonging to low levels, and not of a developing influence socially.

The science of politics, in a civilized community, should have by this time a fine accumulation of simplified knowledge for diffusion in public schools; a store of practical experience in how to promote social advancement most rapidly, a progressive economy and ease of administration, a simplicity in theory and visible benefit in practice, such as should make every child an eager and serviceable citizen.

What do we find, here in America, in the field of "politics?"

We find first a party system which is the technical arrangement to carry on a fight. It is perfectly conceivable that a flourishing democratic government be carried on *without any parties at all;* public functionaries being elected on their merits, and each proposed measure judged on its merits; though this sounds impossible to the androcentric mind.

"There has never been a democracy without factions and parties!" is protested.

There has never been a democracy, so far—only an androcracy.

A group composed of males alone, naturally divides, opposes, fights; even a male church, under the most rigid rule, has its secret undercurrents of antagonism.

"It is the human heart!" is again protested. No, not essentially the human heart, but the male heart. This is so well recognized by men in general, that, to their minds, in this mingled field of politics and warfare, women have no place.

In "civilized warfare" they are, it is true, allowed to trail along and practice their feminine function of nursing; but this is no part of war proper, it is rather the beginning of the end of war. Some time it will strike our "funny spot," these strenuous efforts to hurt and destroy, and these accompanying efforts to heal and save.

But in our politics there is not even provision for a nursing corps; women are absolutely excluded.

"They cannot play the game!" cries the practical politician. There is loud talk of the defilement, the "dirty pool" and its resultant darkening of fair reputations, the total unfitness of lovely woman to take part in "the rough and tumble of politics."

In other words men have made a human institution into an ultra-masculine performance; and, quite rightly, feel that women could not take part in politics *as men do*. That it is not necessary to fulfill this human custom in so masculine a way does not occur to them. Few men can overlook the limitations of their sex and see the truth; that this business of taking care of our common affairs is not only equally open to women and men, but that women are distinctly needed in it.

Anyone will admit that a government wholly in the hands of women would be helped by the assistance of men; that a gynaecocracy must, of its own nature, be one sided. Yet it is hard to win reluctant admission of the opposite fact; that an androcracy must of its own nature be one sided also, and would be greatly improved by the participation of the other sex.

The inextricable confusion of politics and warfare is part of the stumbling block in the minds of men. As they see it, a nation is primarily a fighting organization; and its principal business is offensive and defensive warfare; therefore the ultimatum with which they oppose the demand for political equality—"women cannot fight, therefore they cannot vote."

Fighting, when all is said, is to them the real business of life; not to be able to fight is to be quite out of the running; and ability to solve our growing mass of public problems; questions of health, of education, of morals, of economics; weighs naught against the ability to kill.

This naive assumption of supreme value in a process never of the first importance; and increasingly injurious as society progresses, would be laughable if it were not for its evil effects. It acts and reacts upon us to our hurt. Positively, we see the ill effects already touched on; the evils not only of active war; but of the spirit and methods of war; idealized, inculcated and practiced in other social processes. It tends to make each man-managed nation an actual or potential fighting organization, and to give us, instead of civilized peace, that "balance of power" which is like the counted time in the prize ring—only a rest between combats.

It leaves the weaker nations to be "conquered" and "annexed" just as they used to be; with tariffs instead of tribute. It forces upon each the burden of armament; upon many the dreaded conscription; and continually lowers the world's resources in money and in life.

Similarly in politics, it adds to the legitimate expenses of governing the illegitimate expenses of fighting; and must needs have a "spoils system" by which to pay its mercenaries.

In carrying out the public policies the wheels of state are continually clogged by the "opposition;" always an opposition on one side or the other; and this slow wiggling uneven progress, through shorn victories and haggling concessions, is held to be the proper and only political method.

"Women do not understand politics," we are told; "Women do not care for politics;" "Women are unfitted for politics."

It is frankly inconceivable, from the androcentric view-point, that nations can live in peace together, and be friendly and serviceable as persons are. It is inconceivable also, that in the management of a nation, honesty, efficiency, wisdom, experience and love could work out good results without any element of combat.

The "ultimate resort" is still to arms. "The will of the majority" is only respected on account of the guns of the majority. We have but a partial civilization, heavily modified to sex—the male sex.

WOMAN AND THE STATE

(A Discussion of Political Equality of Men and Women. To be read in connection with chapter 12 of Our Androcentric Culture.)

Here are two vital factors in human life; one a prime essential to our existence; the other a prime essential to our progress.

Both of them we idealize in certain lines, and exploit in others. Both of them are misinterpreted, balked of their full usefulness, and humanity thus injured.

The human race does not get the benefit of the full powers of women, nor of the full powers of the state.

In all civilized races to-day there is a wide and growing sense of discontent among women; a criticism of their assigned limitations, and a demand for larger freedom and opportunity. Under different conditions the demand varies; it is here for higher education, there for justice before the law; here for economic independence, and there for political equality.

This last is at present the most prominent Issue of "the woman question" in England and America, as the activity of the "militant suffragists" has forced it upon the attention of the world.

Thoughtful people in general are now studying this point more seriously than ever before, genuinely anxious to adopt the right side, and there is an alarmed uprising of sincere objection to the political equality of women.

Wasting no time on ignorance, prejudice, or the resistance of special interests, let us fairly face the honest opposition, and do it justice.

The conservative position is this:

"Men and women have different spheres in life. To men belong the creation and management of the state, and the financial maintenance of the home and family:

"To women belong the physical burden of maternity, and the industrial management of the home and family; these duties require all their time and strength:

"The prosperity of the state may be sufficiently conserved by men alone; the prosperity of the family requires the personal presence and services of the mother in the home: if women assume the cares of the state, the home and family will suffer:"

Some go even farther than this, and claim an essential limitation in "the female mind" which prevents it from grasping large political interests; holding, therefore, that if women took part in state affairs it would be to the detriment of the community:

Others advance a theory that "society," in the special sense, is the true sphere of larger service for women, and that those of them not exclusively confined to "home duties" may find full occupation in "social duties," including the time honored fields of "religion" and "charity":

Others again place their main reliance on the statement that, as to the suffrage, "women do not want it."

Let us consider these points in inverse order, beginning with the last one.

We will admit that at present the majority of women are not consciously desirous of any extension of their political rights and privileges, but deny that this indifference is any evidence against the desirability of such extension.

It has long been accepted that the position of women is an index of civilization. Progressive people are proud of the freedom and honor given their women, and our nation honestly believes itself the leader in this line. "American women are the freest in the world!" we say; and boast of it.

Since the agitation for women's rights began, many concessions have been made to further improve their condition. Men, seeing the justice of certain demands, have granted in many states such privileges as admission to schools, colleges, universities, and special instruction for professions; followed by admission to the bar, the pulpit, and the practice of medicine. Married women, in many states, have now a right to their own earnings; and in a few, mothers have an equal right in the guardianship of their children.

We are proud and glad that our women are free to go unveiled, to travel alone, to choose their own husbands; we are proud and glad of every extension of justice already granted by men to women.

Now:—Have any of these concessions been granted because a majority of women asked for them? Was it advanced in opposition to any of them that "women did not want it?" Have as many women ever asked for these things as are now asking for the ballot? If it was desirable to grant these other rights and privileges without the demand of a majority, why is the demand of a majority required before this one is granted?

The child widows of India did not unitedly demand the abolition of the "suttee."

The tortured girl children of China did not rise in overwhelming majority to demand free feet; yet surely no one would refuse to lift these burdens because only a minority of progressive women insisted on justice.

It is a sociological impossibility that a majority of an unorganized class should unite in concerted demand for a right, a duty, which they have never known.

The point to be decided is whether political equality is to the advantage of women and of the state—not whether either, as a body, is asking for it.

Now for the "society" theory. There is a venerable fiction to the effect that women make—and manage, "society." No careful student of comparative history can hold this belief for a moment. Whatever the conditions of the age or place; industrial, financial, religious, political, educational; these conditions are in the hands of men; and these conditions dictate the "society" of that age or place.

"Society" in a constitutional monarchy is one thing; in a primitive despotism another; among millionaires a third; but women do not make the despotism, the monarchy, or the millions. They take social conditions as provided by men, precisely as they take all other conditions at their hands. They do not even modify an existing society to their own interests, being powerless to do so. The "double standard of morals," ruling everywhere in "society," proves this; as does the comparative helplessness of women to enjoy even social entertainments, without the constant attendance and invitation of men.

Even in its great function of exhibition leading to marriage, it is the girls who are trained and exhibited, under closest surveillance; while the men stroll in and out, to chose at will, under no surveillance whatever.

That women, otherwise powerful, may use "society" to further their ends, is as true as that men do; and in England, where women, through their titled and landed position, have always had more political power than here, "society" is a very useful vehicle for the activities of both sexes.

But, in the main, the opportunities of "society" to women, are merely opportunities to use their "feminine influence" in extra domestic lines—a very questionable advantage to the home and family, to motherhood, to women, or to the state.

In religion women have always filled and more than filled the place allowed them. Needless to say it was a low one. The power of the church, its whole management and emoluments, were always in the hands of men, save when the Lady Abbess held her partial sway; but the work of the church has always been helped by women—the men have preached and the women practised!

Charity, as a vocation, is directly in line with the mother instinct, and has always appealed to women. Since we have learned how injurious to true social development this mistaken kindness is, it might almost be classified as a morbid by-product of suppressed femininity!

In passing we may note that charity as a virtue is ranked highest among those nations and religions where women are held lowest. With the Moslems it is a universal law—and in the Moslem Paradise there are no women—save the Houries!

The playground of a man-fenced "society"; the work-ground of a man-taught church; and this "osmosis" of social nutrition, this leakage and seepage of values which should circulate normally, called charity; these are not a sufficient field for the activities of women.

As for those limitations of the "feminine mind" which render her unfit to consider the victuallage of a nation, or the justice of a tax on sugar; it hardly seems as if the charge need be taken seriously. Yet so able a woman as Mrs. Humphry Ward has recently advanced it in all earnestness.

In her view women are capable of handling municipal, but not state affairs. Since even this was once denied them; and since, in England, they have had municipal suffrage for some time; it would seem as if their abilities grew with use, as most abilities do; which is in truth the real answer.

Most women spend their whole lives, and have spent their whole lives for uncounted generations, in the persistent and exclusive contemplation of their own family affairs. They are near-sighted, or near-minded, rather; the trouble is not with the nature of their minds, but with the use of them.

If men as a class had been exclusively confined to the occupation of house-service since history began, they would be similarly unlikely to manifest an acute political intelligence.

We may agree with Tennyson that "Woman is not undeveloped man, but diverse;" that is *women* are not undeveloped *men;* but the feminine half of humanity is undeveloped human. They have exercised their feminine functions, but not their human-functions; at least not to their full extent.

Here appears a distinction which needs to be widely appreciated.

We are not merely male and female—all animals are that—our chief distinction is that of race, our humanness.

Male characteristics we share with all males, bird and beast; female characteristics we share with all females, similarly; but human characteristics belong to *genus homo* alone; and are possessed by both sexes. A female horse is just as much a horse as a male of her species; a female human being is just as human as the male of her species—or ought to be!

In the special functions and relations of sex there is no contest, no possible rivalry or confusion; but in the general functions of humanity there is great misunderstanding.

Our trouble is that we have not recognized these human functions as such; but supposed them to be exclusively masculine; and, acting under that idea, strove to prevent women from an unnatural imitation of men.

Hence this minor theory of the limitations of the "female mind."

The mind is pre-eminently human. That degree of brain development which distinguishes our species, is a human, not a sex characteristic.

There may be, has been, and still is, a vast difference in our treatment of the minds of the two sexes. We have given them a different education, different exercises, different conditions in all ways. But all these differences are external, and their effect disappears with them.

The "female mind" has proven its identical capacity with the "male mind," *in so far as it has been given identical conditions.* It will take a long time, however, before conditions are so identical, for successive generations, as to give the "female mind" a fair chance.

In the meantime, considering its traditional, educational and associative drawbacks, the "female mind" has made a remarkably good showing.

The field of politics is an unfortunate one in which to urge this alleged limitation; because politics is one of the few fields in which some women have been reared and exercised under equal conditions with men.

We have had queens as long as we have had kings, perhaps longer; and history does not show the male mind, in kings, to have manifested a numerically proportionate superiority over the female mind, in queens.

There have been more kings than queens, but have there been more good and great ones, in proportion?

Even one practical and efficient queen is proof enough that being a woman does not preclude political capacity. Since England has had such an able queen for so long, and that within Mrs. Humphry Ward's personal memory, her position seems fatuous in the extreme.

It has been advanced that great queens owed their power to the association and advice of the noble and high-minded men who surrounded them; and, further, that the poor showing made by many kings, was due to the association and vice of the base and low-minded women who surrounded them.

This is a particularly pusillanimous claim in the first place; is not provable in the second place; and, if it were true, opens up a very pretty field of study in the third place. It would seem to prove, if it proves anything, that men are not fit to be trusted with political power on account of an alarming affinity for the worst of women; and, conversely, that women, as commanding the assistance of the best of men, are visibly the right rulers! Also it opens a pleasant sidelight on that oft-recommended tool—"feminine influence."

We now come to our opening objection; that society and state, home, and family, are best served by the present division of interests: and its corollary, that if women enlarge that field of interest it would reduce their usefulness in their present sphere.

The corollary is easily removed. We are now on the broad ground of established facts; of history, recent, but still achieved.

Women have had equal political rights with men in several places, for considerable periods of time. In Wyoming, to come near home, they have enjoyed this status for more than a generation. Neither here nor in any other state or country where women vote, is there the faintest proof of injury to the home or family relation. In Wyoming, indeed, divorce has decreased, while gaining so fast in other places.

Political knowledge, political interest, does not take up more time and strength than any other form of mental activity; nor does it preclude a keen efficiency in other lines; and as for the actual time required to perform the average duties of citizenship—it is a contemptible bit of trickery in argument, if not mere ignorance and confusion of idea, to urge the occasional attendance on political meetings, or the annual or bi-annual dropping of a ballot, as any interference with the management of a house.

It is proven, by years on years of established experience, that women can enjoy full political equality and use their power, without in the least ceasing to be contented and efficient wives and mothers, cooks and housekeepers.

What really horrifies the popular mind at the thought of women in politics, is the picture of woman as a "practical politician;" giving her time to it as a business, and making money by it, in questionable, or unquestionable, ways; and, further, as a politician in office, as sheriff, alderman, senator, judge.

The popular mind becomes suffused with horror at the first idea, and scarcely less so at the second. It pictures blushing girlhood on the Bench; tender motherhood in the Senate; the housewife turned "ward-heeler;" and becomes quite sick in contemplation of these abominations.

No educated mind, practical mind, no mind able and willing to use its faculties, need be misled for a moment by these sophistries.

There is absolutely no evidence that women as a class will rush into "practical politics." Where they have voted longest they do not manifest this dread result. Neither is there any proof that they will all desire to hold office; or that any considerable portion of them will; or that, if they did, they would get it.

We seem unconsciously to assume that when women begin to vote, men will stop; or that the women will outnumber the men; also that, outnumbering them, they will be completely united in their vote; and, still further, that so outnumbering and uniting, they will solidly vote for a ticket composed wholly of women candidates.

Does anyone seriously imagine this to be likely?

This may be stated with assurance; if ever we do see a clever, designing, flirtatious, man-twisting woman; or a pretty, charming, irresistable young girl, elected to office—it will not be by the votes of women!

Where women are elected to office, by the votes of both men and women, they are of suitable age and abilities, and do their work well. They have already greatly improved some of the conditions of local politics, and the legislation they advocate is of a beneficial character.

What is the true relation of women to the state?

It is precisely identical with that of men. Their forms of service may vary, but their duty, their interest, their responsibility, is the same.

Here are the people on earth, half of them women, all of them her children. It is her earth as much as his; the people are their people, the state their state; compounded of them all, in due relation.

As the father and mother, together; shelter, guard, teach and provide for their children in the home; so should all fathers and mothers, together; shelter, guard, teach and provide for their common children, the community.

The state is no mystery; no taboo place of masculine secrecy; it is simply us.

Democracy is but a half-grown child as yet, one of twins? Its boy-half is a struggling thing, with "the diseases of babyhood"; its girl-half has hardly begun to take notice.

As human creatures we have precisely the same duty and privilege, interest, and power in the state; sharing its protection, its advantages, and its services. As women we have a different relation.

Here indeed we will admit, and glory in, our "diversity." The "eternal womanly" is a far more useful thing in the state than the "eternal manly."

To be woman means to be mother. To be mother means to give love, defense, nourishment, care, instruction. Too long, far too long has motherhood neglected its real social duties, its duties to humanity at large. Even in her position of retarded industrial development, as the housekeeper and houseworker of the world, woman has a contribution of special value to the state.

As the loving mother, the patient teacher, the tender nurse, the wise provider and care-taker, she can serve the state, and the state needs her service.

XIII

Industry and Economics

The forest of Truth, on the subject of industry and economics, is difficult to see on account of the trees.

We have so many Facts on this subject; so many Opinions; so many Traditions and Habits; and the pressure of Immediate Conclusions is so intense upon us all; that it is not easy to form a clear space in one's mind and consider the field fairly.

Possibly the present treatment of the subject will appeal most to the minds of those who know least about it; such as the Average Woman. To her, Industry is a daylong and lifelong duty, as well as a natural impulse; and economics means going without things. To such untrained but also unprejudiced minds it should be easy to show the main facts on these lines.

Let us dispose of Economics first, as having a solemn scientific appearance.

Physical Economics treats of the internal affairs of the body; the whole machinery and how it works; all organs, members, functions; each last and littlest capillary and leucocyte, are parts of that "economy."

Nature's "economy" is not in the least "economical." The waste of life, the waste of material, the waste of time and effort, are prodigious, yet she achieves her end as we see.

Domestic Economics covers the whole care and government of the household; the maintenance of peace, health, order, and morality; the care and nourishment of children as far as done at home; the entire management of the home, as well as the spending and saving of money; are included in it. Saving is the least and poorest part of it; especially as in mere abstinence from needed things; most especially when this abstinence is mainly "Mother's." How best to spend; time, strength, love, care, labor, knowledge, and money—this should be the main study in Domestic Economics.

Social, or, as they are used to call it, Political Economics, covers a larger, but not essentially different field. A family consists of people, and the Mother is their natural manager. Society consists of people— *the same people*—only more of them. All the people, who are members of Society, are also members of families—except some incubated orphans maybe. Social Economics covers the whole care and management of the people, the maintenance of peace and health and order and morality; the care of children, as far as done out of the home; as well as the spending and saving of the public money—all these are included in it.

This great business of Social Economics is at present little understood and most poorly managed, for this reason; we approach it from an individual point of view; seeking not so much to do our share in the common service, as to get our personal profit from the common wealth. Where the whole family labors together to harvest fruit and store it for the winter, we have legitimate Domestic Economics: but where one member takes and hides a lot for himself, to the exclusion of the others, we have no Domestic Economics at all—merely individual selfishness.

In Social Economics we have a large, but simple problem. Here is the earth, our farm. Here are the people, who own the earth. How can the most advantage to the most people be obtained from the earth with the least labor? That is the problem of Social Economics.

Looking at the world as if you held it in your hands to study and discuss, what do we find at present?

We find people living too thickly for health and comfort in some places, and too thinly for others; we find most people working too hard and too long at honest labor; some people working with damaging intensity at dishonest labor; and a few wretched paupers among the rich and poor, degenerate idlers who do not work at all, the scum and the dregs of Society.

All this is bad economics. We do not get the comfort out of life we easily could; and work far too hard for what we do get. Moreover, there is no peace, no settled security. No man is sure of his living, no matter how hard he works, a thousand things may occur to deprive him of his job, or his income. In our time there is great excitement along this line of study; and more than one proposition is advanced whereby we may improve, most notably instanced in the world-covering advance of Socialism.

In our present study the principal fact to be exhibited is the influence of a male culture upon Social Economics and Industry.

Industry, as a department of Social Economics, is little understood. Heretofore we have viewed this field from several wholly erroneous positions. From the Hebrew (and wholly androcentric) religious teaching, we have regarded labor as a curse.

Nothing could be more absurdly false. Labor is not merely a means of supporting human life—it *is* human life. Imagine a race of beings living without labor! They must be the rudest savages.

Human work consists in specialized industry and the exchange of its products; and without it is no civilization. As industry develops, civilization develops; peace expands; wealth increases; science and art help on the splendid total. Productive industry, and its concomitant of distributive industry cover the major field of human life.

If our industry was normal, what should we see?

A world full of healthy, happy people; each busily engaged in what he or she most enjoys doing. Normal Specialization, like all our voluntary processes, is accompanied by keen pleasure; and any check or interruption to it gives pain and injury. Whosoever works at what he loves is well and happy. Whoso works at what he does not love is ill and miserable. It is very bad economics to force unwilling industry. That is the weakness of slave labor; and of wage labor also where there is not full industrial education and freedom of choice.

Under normal conditions we should see well developed, well trained specialists happily engaged in the work they most enjoyed; for reasonable hours (any work, or play either, becomes injurious if done too long); and as a consequence the whole output of the world would be vastly improved, not only in quantity but in quality.

Plain are the melancholy facts of what we do see. Following that pitiful conception of labor as a curse, comes the very old and androcentric habit of despising it as belonging to women, and then to slaves.

As a matter of fact industry is in its origin feminine; that is, maternal. It is the overflowing fountain of mother-love and mother-power which first prompts the human race to labor; and for long ages men performed no productive industry at all; being merely hunters and fighters.

It is this lack of natural instinct for labor in the male of our species, together with the ideas and opinions based on that lack, and voiced by him in his many writings, religious and other, which have given to the world its false estimate of this great function, human work. That which is our very life, our greatest joy, our road to all advancement, we have scorned and oppressed; so that "working people," the "working classes," "having to work," etc., are to this day spoken of with contempt. Perhaps drones speak so among themselves of the "working bees!"

Normally, widening out from the mother's careful and generous service in the family, to careful, generous service in the world, we should find labor freely given, with love and pride.

Abnormally, crushed under the burden of androcentric scorn and prejudice, we have labor grudgingly produced under pressure of necessity; labor of slaves under fear of the whip, or of wage-slaves, one step higher, under fear of want. Long ages wherein hunting and fighting were the only manly occupations, have left their heavy impress. The predacious instinct and the combative instinct weigh down and disfigure our economic development. What Veblen calls "the instinct of workmanship" grows on, slowly and irresistably; but the malign features of our industrial life are distinctively androcentric: the desire to get, of the hunter; interfering with the desire to give, of the mother; the desire to overcome an antagonist—originally masculine, interfering with the desire to serve and benefit—originally feminine.

Let the reader keep in mind that as human beings, men are able to over-live their masculine natures and do noble service to the world; also that as human beings they are today far more highly developed than women, and doing far more for the world. The point here brought out is that as males their unchecked supremacy has resulted in the abnormal predominance of masculine impulses in our human processes; and that this predominance has been largely injurious.

As it happens, the distinctly feminine or maternal impulses are far more nearly in line with human progress than are those of the male; which makes her exclusion from human functions the more mischievous.

Our current teachings in the infant science of Political Economy are naively masculine. They assume as unquestionable that "the economic man" will never do anything unless he has to; will only do it to escape pain or attain pleasure; and will, inevitably, take all he can get, and do all he can to outwit, overcome, and if necessary destroy his antagonist.

Always the antagonist; to the male mind an antagonist is essential to progress, to all achievement. He has planted that root-thought in all the human world; from that old hideous idea of Satan, "The Adversary," down to the competitor in business, or the boy at the head of the class, to be superseded by another.

Therefore, even in science, "the struggle for existence" is the dominant law—to the male mind, with the "survival of the fittest" and "the elimination of the unfit."

Therefore in industry and economics we find always and everywhere the antagonist; the necessity for somebody or something to be overcome—else why make an effort? If you have not the incentive of reward, or the incentive of combat, why work? "Competition is the life of trade."

Thus the Economic Man.

But how about the Economic Woman?

To the androcentric mind she does not exist. Women are females, and that's all; their working abilities are limited to personal service.

That it would be possible to develop industry to far greater heights, and to find in social economics a simple and beneficial process for the promotion of human life and prosperity, under any other impulse than these two, Desire and Combat, is hard indeed to recognize—for the "male mind."

So absolutely interwoven are our existing concepts of maleness and humanness, so sure are we that men are people and women only females, that the claim of equal weight and dignity in human affairs of the feminine instincts and methods is scouted as absurd. We find existing industry almost wholly in male hands; find it done as men do it; assume that that is the way it must be done.

When women suggest that it could be done differently, their proposal is waved aside—they are "only women"—their ideas are "womanish."

Agreed. So are men "only men," their ideas are "mannish"; and of the two the women are more vitally human than the men.

The female is the race-type—the man the variant.

The female, as a race-type, having the female processes besides; best performs the race processes. The male, however, has with great difficulty developed them, always heavily handicapped by his maleness; being in origin essentially a creature of sex, and so dominated almost exclusively by sex impulses.

The human instinct of mutual service is checked by the masculine instinct of combat; the human tendency to specialize in labor, to rejoicingly pour force in lines of specialized expression, is checked by the predacious instinct, which will exert itself for reward; and disfigured by the masculine instinct of self-expression, which is an entirely different thing from the great human outpouring of world force.

Great men, the world's teachers and leaders, are great in humanness; mere maleness does not make for greatness unless it be in warfare—a disadvantageous glory! Great women also must be great in humanness; but their female instincts are not so subversive of human progress as are the instincts of the male. To be a teacher and leader, to love and serve, to guard and guide and help, are well in line with motherhood.

"Are they not also in line with fatherhood?" will be asked; and, "Are not the father's paternal instincts masculine?"

No, they are not; they differ in no way from the maternal, in so far as they are beneficial. Parental functions of the higher sort, of the human sort, are identical. The father can give his children many advantages which the mother can not; but that is due to his superiority as a human being. He possesses far more knowledge and power in the world, the human world; he himself is more developed in human powers and processes; and is therefore able to do much for his children which the mother can not; but this is in no way due to his masculinity. It is in this development of human powers in man, through fatherhood, that we may read the explanation of our short period of androcentric culture.

So thorough and complete a reversal of previous relation, such continuance of what appears in every way an unnatural position, must have had some justification in racial advantages, or it could not have endured. This is its justification; the establishment of humanness in the male; he being led into it, along natural lines, by the exercise of previously existing desires.

In a male culture the attracting forces must inevitably have been, we have seen, Desire and Combat. These masculine forces, acting upon human processes, while necessary to the uplifting of the man, have been anything but uplifting to civilization. A sex which thinks, feels and acts in terms of combat is difficult to harmonize in the smooth bonds of human relationship; that they have succeeded so well is a beautiful testimony to the superior power of race tendency over sex tendency. Uniting and organizing, crudely and temporarily, for the common hunt; and then, with progressive elaboration, for the common fight; they are now using the same tactics—and the same desires, unfortunately—in common work.

Union, organization, complex interservice, are the essential processes of a growing society; in them, in the ever-increasing discharge of power along widening lines of action, is the joy and health of social life. But so far men combine in order to better combat; the mutual service held incidental to the common end of conquest and plunder.

In spite of this the overmastering power of humanness is now developing among modern men immense organizations of a wholly beneficial character, with no purpose but mutual advantage. This is true human growth, and as such will inevitably take the place of the sex-prejudiced earlier processes.

The human character of the Christian religion is now being more and more insisted on; the practical love and service of each and all; in place of the old insistence on Desire—for a Crown and Harp in Heaven, and Combat—with that everlasting adversary.

In economics this great change is rapidly going on before our eyes. It is a change in idea, in basic concept, in our theory of what the whole thing is about. We are beginning to see the world, not as "a fair field and no favor"—not a place for one man to get ahead of others, for a price; but as an establishment belonging to us, the proceeds of which are to be applied, as a matter of course, to human advantage.

In the old idea, the wholly masculine idea, based on the processes of sex-combat, the advantage of the world lay in having "the best man win." Some, in the first steps of enthusiasm for Eugenics, think so still; imagining that the primal process of promoting evolution through the paternity of the conquering male is the best process.

To have one superior lion kill six or sixty inferior lions, and leave a progeny of more superior lions behind him, is all right—for lions; the superiority in fighting being all the superiority they need.

But the man able to outwit his follows, to destroy them in physical, or ruin in financial, combat, is not therefore a superior human creature. Even physical superiority, as a fighter, does not prove the kind of vigor best calculated to resist disease, or to adapt itself to changing conditions.

That our masculine culture in its effect on Economics and Industry is injurious, is clearly shown by the whole open page of history. From the simple beneficent activities of a matriarchal period we follow the same lamentable steps; nation after nation. Women are enslaved and captives are enslaved; a military despotism is developed; labor is despised and discouraged. Then when the irresistible social forces do bring us onward, in science, art, commerce, and all that we call civilization, we find the same check acting always upon that progress; and the really vital social processes of production and distribution heavily injured by the financial combat and carnage which rages ever over and among them.

The real development of the people, the forming of finer physiques, finer minds, a higher level of efficiency, a broader range of enjoyment and accomplishment—is hindered and not helped by this artificially maintained "struggle for existence," this constant endeavor to eliminate what, from a masculine standard, is "unfit."

That we have progressed thus far, that we are now moving forward so rapidly, is in spite of and not because of our androcentric culture.

XIV

A HUMAN WORLD

In the change from the dominance of one sex to the equal power of two, to what may we look forward? What effect upon civilization is to be expected from the equality of womanhood in the human race?

To put the most natural question first—what will men lose by it? Many men are genuinely concerned about this; fearing some new position of subservience and disrespect. Others laugh at the very idea of change in their position, relying as always on the heavier fist. So long as fighting was the determining process, the best fighter must needs win; but in the rearrangement of processes which marks our age, superior physical strength does not make the poorer wealthy, nor even the soldier a general.

The major processes of life to-day are quite within the powers of women; women are fulfilling their new relations more and more successfully; gathering new strength, new knowledge, new ideals. The change is upon us; what will it do to men?

No harm.

As we are a monogamous race, there will be no such drastic and cruel selection among competing males as would eliminate the vast majority as unfit. Even though some be considered unfit for fatherhood, all human life remains open to them. Perhaps the most important feature of this change comes in right here; along this old line of sex-selection, replacing that power in the right hands, and using it for the good of the race.

The woman, free at last, intelligent, recognizing her real place and responsibility in life as a human being, will be not less, but more, efficient as a mother. She will understand that, in the line of physical evolution, motherhood is the highest process; and that her work, as a contribution to an improved race, must always involve this great function. She will see that right parentage is the purpose of the whole scheme of sex-relationship, and act accordingly.

In our time, his human faculties being sufficiently developed, civilized man can look over and around his sex limitations, and begin to see what are the true purposes and methods of human life.

He is now beginning to learn that his own governing necessity of Desire is not *the* governing necessity of parentage, but only a contributory tendency; and that, in the interests of better parentage, motherhood is the dominant factor, and must be so considered.

In slow reluctant admission of this fact, man heretofore has recognized one class of women as mothers; and has granted them a varying amount of consideration as such; but he has none the less insisted on maintaining another class of women, forbidden motherhood, and merely subservient to his desires; a barren, mischievous unnatural relation, wholly aside from parental purposes, and absolutely injurious to society. This whole field of morbid action will be eliminated from human life by the normal development of women.

It is not a question of interfering with or punishing men; still less of interfering with or punishing women; but purely a matter of changed education and opportunity for every child.

Each and all shall be taught the real nature and purpose of motherhood; the real nature and purpose of manhood; what each is for, and which is the more important. A new sense of the power and pride of womanhood will waken; a womanhood no longer sunk in helpless dependence upon men; no longer limited to mere unpaid house-service; no longer blinded by the false morality which subjects even motherhood to man's dominance; but a womanhood which will recognize its pre-eminent responsibility to the human race, and live up to it. Then, with all normal and right competition among men for the favor of women, those best fitted for fatherhood will be chosen. Those who are not chosen will live single—perforce.

Many, under the old mistaken notion of what used to be called the "social necessity" of prostitution, will protest at the idea of its extinction.

"It is necessary to have it," they will say.

"Necessary *to whom?*"

Not to the women hideously sacrificed to it, surely.

Not to society, honey-combed with diseases due to this cause.

Not to the family, weakened and impoverished by it.

To whom then? To the men who want it?

But it is not good for them, it promotes all manner of disease, of vice, of crime. It is absolutely and unquestionably a "social evil."

An intelligent and powerful womanhood will put an end to this indulgence of one sex at the expense of the other; and to the injury of both.

In this inevitable change will lie what some men will consider a loss. But only those of the present generation. For the sons of the women now entering upon this new era of world life will be differently reared. They will recognize the true relation of men to the primal process; and be amazed that for so long the greater values have been lost sight of in favor of the less.

This one change will do more to promote the physical health and beauty of the race; to improve the quality of children born, and the general vigor and purity of social life, than any one measure which could be proposed. It rests upon a recognition of motherhood as the real base and cause of the family; and dismisses to the limbo of all outworn superstition that false Hebraic and grossly androcentric doctrine that the woman is to be subject to the man, and that he shall rule over her. He has tried this arrangement long enough—to the grievous injury of the world. A higher standard of happiness will result; equality and mutual respect between parents; pure love, undefiled by self-interests on either side; and a new respect for Childhood.

With the Child, seen at last to be the governing purpose of this relation, with all the best energies of men and women bent on raising the standard of life for all children, we shall have a new status of family life which will be clean and noble, and satisfying to all its members.

The change in all the varied lines of human work is beyond the powers of any present day prophet to forecast with precision. A new grade of womanhood we can clearly foresee; proud, strong, serene, independent; great mothers of great women and great men. These will hold high standards and draw men up to them; by no compulsion save nature's law of attraction. A clean and healthful world, enjoying the taste of life as it never has since racial babyhood, with homes of quiet and content—this we can foresee.

Art—in the extreme sense will perhaps always belong most to men. It would seem as if that ceaseless urge to expression, was, at least originally, most congenial to the male. But applied art, in every form, and art used directly for transmission of ideas, such as literature, or oratory, appeals to women as much, if not more, than to men.

We can make no safe assumption as to what, if any, distinction there will be in the free human work of men and women, until we have seen generation after generation grow up under absolutely equal conditions. In all our games and sports and minor social customs, such changes will occur as must needs follow upon the rising dignity alloted to the woman's temperament, the woman's point of view; not in the least denying to men the fullest exercise of their special powers and preferences; but classifying these newly, as not human—merely male. At present we have pages or columns in our papers, marked as "The Woman's Page" "Of Interest to Women," and similar delimiting titles. Similarly we might have distinctly masculine matters so marked and specified; not assumed as now to be of general human interest.

The effect of the change upon Ethics and Religion is deep and wide. With the entrance of women upon full human life, a new principle comes into prominence; the principle of loving service. That this is the governing principle of Christianity is believed by many; but an androcentric interpretation has quite overlooked it; and made, as we have shown, the essential dogma of their faith the desire of an eternal reward and the combat with an eternal enemy.

The feminine attitude in life is wholly different. As a female she has merely to be herself and passively attract; neither to compete nor to pursue; as a mother her whole process is one of growth; first the development of the live child within her, and the wonderful nourishment from her own body; and then all the later cultivation to make the child grow; all the watching, teaching, guarding, feeding. In none of this is there either desire, combat, or self-expression. The feminine attitude, as expressed in religion, makes of it a patient practical fulfillment of law; a process of large sure improvements; a limitless comforting love and care.

This full assurance of love and of power; this endless cheerful service; the broad provision for all people; rather than the competitive selection of a few "victors;" is the natural presentation of religious truth from the woman's viewpoint. Her governing principle being growth and not combat; her main tendency being to give and not to get; she more easily and naturally lives and teaches these religious principles. It is for this reason that the broader gentler teaching of the Unitarian and Universalist sects have appealed so especially to women, and that so many women preach in their churches.

This principle of growth, as applied and used in general human life will work to far other ends than those now so painfully visible.

In education, for instance, with neither reward nor punishment as spur or bait; with no competition to rouse effort and animosity, but rather with the feeling of a gardener towards his plants; the teacher will teach and the children learn, in mutual ease and happiness. The law of passive attraction applies here, leading to such ingenuity in presentation as shall arouse the child's interest; and, in the true spirit of promoting growth, each child will have his best and fullest training, without regard to who is "ahead" of him, or her, or who "behind."

We do not sadly measure the cabbage-stalk by the corn-stalk, and praise the corn for getting ahead of the cabbage—nor incite the cabbage to emulate the corn. We nourish both, to its best growth—and are the richer.

That every child on earth shall have right conditions to make the best growth possible to it; that every citizen, from birth to death, shall have a chance to learn all he or she can assimilate, to develop every power that is in them—for the common good—this will be the aim of education, under human management.

In the world of "society" we may look for very radical changes.

With all women full human beings, trained and useful in some form of work; the class of busy idlers, who run about forever "entertaining" and being "entertained" will disappear as utterly as will the prostitute. No woman with real work to do could have the time for such petty amusements; or enjoy them if she did have time. No woman with real work to do, work she loved and was well fitted for, work honored and well-paid, would take up the Unnatural Trade. Genuine relaxation and recreation, all manner of healthful sports and pastimes, beloved of both sexes to-day, will remain, of course; but the set structure of "social functions"—so laughably misnamed—will disappear with the "society women" who make it possible. Once active members of real Society; no woman could go back to "society," any more than a roughrider could return to a hobbyhorse.

New development in dress, wise, comfortable, beautiful, may be confidently expected, as woman becomes more human. No fully human creature could hold up its head under the absurdities our women wear to-day—and have worn for dreary centuries.

So on through all the aspects of life we may look for changes, rapid and far-reaching; but natural and all for good. The improvement is not due to any inherent moral superiority of women; nor to any moral inferiority of men; men at present, as more human, are ahead of women in all distinctly human ways; yet their maleness, as we have shown repeatedly, warps and disfigures their humanness. The woman, being by nature the race-type; and her feminine functions being far more akin to human functions than are those essential to the male; will bring into human life a more normal influence.

Under this more normal influence our present perversities of functions will, of course, tend to disappear. The directly serviceable tendency of women, as shown in every step of their public work, will have small patience with hoary traditions of absurdity. We need but look at long recorded facts to see what women do—or try to do, when they have opportunity. Even in their crippled, smothered past, they have made valiant efforts—not always wise—in charity and philanthropy.

In our own time this is shown through all the length and breadth of our country, by the Woman's Clubs. Little groups of women, drawing together in human relation, at first, perhaps, with no better purpose than to "improve their minds," have grown and spread; combined and federated; and in their great reports, representing hundreds of thousands of women—we find a splendid record of human work. They strive always to improve something, to take care of something, to help and serve and benefit. In "village improvement," in traveling libraries, in lecture courses and exhibitions, in promoting good legislation; in many a line of noble effort our Women's Clubs show what women want to do.

Men do not have to do these things through their clubs, which are mainly for pleasure; they can accomplish what they wish to through regular channels. But the character and direction of the influence of women in human affairs is conclusively established by the things they already do and try to do. In those countries, and in our own states, where they are already full citizens, the legislation introduced and promoted by them is of the same beneficent character. The normal woman is a strong creature, loving and serviceable. The kind of woman men are afraid to entrust with political power, selfish, idle, over-sexed, or ignorant and narrow-minded, is not normal, but is the creature of conditions men have made. We need have no fear of her, for she will disappear with the conditions which created her.

In older days, without knowledge of the natural sciences, we accepted life as static. If, being born in China, we grew up with foot-bound women, we assumed that women were such, and must so remain. Born in India, we accepted the child-wife, the pitiful child-widow, the ecstatic *suttee*, as natural expressions of womanhood. In each age, each country, we have assumed life to be necessarily what it was—a moveless fact.

All this is giving way fast in our new knowledge of the laws of life. We find that Growth is the eternal law, and that even rocks are slowly changing. Human life is seen to be as dynamic as any other form; and the most certain thing about it is that it will change. In the light of this knowledge we need no longer accept the load of what we call "sin;" the grouped misery of poverty, disease and crime; the cumbrous, inefficacious, wasteful processes of life today, as needful or permanent.

We have but to learn the *real* elements in humanity; its true powers and natural characteristics; to see wherein we are hampered by the wrong ideas and inherited habits of earlier generations, and break loose from them—then we can safely and swiftly introduce a far nobler grade of living.

Of all crippling hindrances in false ideas, we have none more universally mischievous than this root error about men and women. Given the old androcentric theory, and we have an androcentric culture—the kind we so far know; this short stretch we call "history;" with its proud and pitiful record. We have done wonders of upward growth—for growth is the main law, and may not be wholly resisted. But we have hindered, perverted, temporarily checked that growth, age after age; and again and again has a given nation, far advanced and promising, sunk to ruin, and left another to take up its task of social evolution; repeat its errors—and its failure.

One major cause of the decay of nations is "the social evil"—a thing wholly due to the androcentric culture. Another steady endless check is warfare—due to the same cause. Largest of all is poverty; that spreading disease which grows with our social growth and shows most horribly when and where we are most proud, keeping step, as it were, with private wealth. This too, in large measure, is due to the false ideas on industry and economics, based, like the others mentioned, on a wholly masculine view of life.

By changing our underlying theory in this matter we change all the resultant assumptions; and it is this alteration in our basic theory of life which is being urged.

The scope and purpose of human life is entirely above and beyond the field of sex relationship. Women are human beings, as much as men, by nature; and as women, are even more sympathetic with human processes. To develop human life in its true powers we need full equal citizenship for women.

The great woman's movement and labor movement of to-day are parts of the same pressure, the same world-progress. An economic democracy must rest on a free womanhood; and a free womanhood inevitably leads to an economic democracy.

A Note About the Author

Charlotte Perkins Gilman (1860–1935) was an American author, feminist, and social reformer. Born in Hartford, Connecticut, Gilman was raised by her mother after her father abandoned his family to poverty. A single mother, Mary Perkins struggled to provide for her son and daughter, frequently enlisting the help of her estranged husband's aunts, including Harriet Beecher Stowe, the author of *Uncle Tom's Cabin*. These early experiences shaped Charlotte's outlook on gender and society, inspiring numerous written works and a lifetime of activism. Gilman excelled in school as a youth and went on to study at the Rhode Island School of Design where, in 1879, she met a woman named Martha Luther. The two were involved romantically for the next few years until Luther married in 1881. Distraught, Gilman eventually married Charles Walter Stetson, a painter, in 1884, with whom she had one daughter. After Katharine's birth, Gilman suffered an intense case of post-partum depression, an experience which inspired her landmark story "The Yellow Wallpaper" (1890). Gilman and Stetson divorced in 1894, after which Charlotte moved to California and became active in social reform. Gilman was a pioneer of the American feminist movement and an early advocate for women's suffrage, divorce, and euthanasia. Her radical beliefs and controversial views on race—Gilman was known to support white supremacist ideologies—nearly consigned her work to history; at the time of her death none of her works remained in print. In the 1970s, however, the rise of second-wave feminism and its influence on literary scholarship revived her reputation, bringing her work back into publication.

A Note from the Publisher

Spanning many genres, from non-fiction essays to literature classics to children's books and lyric poetry, Mint Edition books showcase the master works of our time in a modern new package. The text is freshly typeset, is clean and easy to read, and features a new note about the author in each volume. Many books also include exclusive new introductory material. Every book boasts a striking new cover, which makes it as appropriate for collecting as it is for gift giving. Mint Edition books are only printed when a reader orders them, so natural resources are not wasted. We're proud that our books are never manufactured in excess and exist only in the exact quantity they need to be read and enjoyed. To learn more and view our library, go to minteditionbooks.com

 **MINT EDITIONS**

Enjoy more of your favorite classics with Bookfinity,
a new search and discovery experience for readers.
With Bookfinity, you can discover more vintage
literature for your collection, find your Reader Type,
track books you've read or want to read,
and add reviews to your favorite books.
Visit www.bookfinity.com, and click on
Take the Quiz to get started.

Don't forget to follow us
@bookfinityofficial and @mint_editions